SHADOW ASPECTS

Of Self And How I Healed

SUSHMITA CHOUDHURY

notionpress
.com

INDIA • SINGAPORE • MALAYSIA

ISBN 979-8-89026-728-3

WHAT IS SHADOW?

Before we leap into knowing how I healed or how one can heal the shadow aspects of life, through the enormous mind of Veteran Writers, let's dive into knowing what the shadow aspects of self are. I take to quote, with all due respect, the legendary figure CARL JUNG and Nobel Prize winner ALEKSANDR SOLZHENITSYN.

"The shadow is a moral problem that challenges the whole ego-personality, for no one can become conscious of the shadow without considerable moral effort. To become conscious of the shadow self it involves recognizing the dark aspects of the personality as present and real. This act is the essential condition for any kind of self-knowledge."

– Carl Jung, Aion (1951)

"Filling the conscious mind with ideal conceptions is a characteristic of Western theosophy, but not the confrontation with the shadow self and the world of darkness. One does not become enlightened by imagining figures of light, but by making the darkness conscious."

– Carl Jung, Alchemical Studies (1945)

"If only it were all so simple! If only there were evil people somewhere insidiously committing evil deeds, and it were necessary only to separate them from the rest of us and destroy them. But the line dividing good and evil cuts through the heart of every human being. And who is willing to destroy a piece of his own heart?"

– Aleksandr Solzhenitsyn

CONTENTS

THE FATED MEETING

This is about *June* 2019,

Escaping from the summer heat, I traveled to Nainital for a week. I desperately needed a change from the monotonous lifestyle I was leading. I asked my family to schedule a trip, but none of them were interested. I decided to travel alone as they were all tied up with their busy schedule.

I reached the pre-booked Hotel around mid-noon, and as I got down from the car, a cool breeze chafed me with the freshness of the mountains. I felt the touch of such calmness after many years. It was drizzling. I walked up to the Man at the reception desk and he welcomed me with a beaming smile on his face. He handed over to me, the key to my room and helped me to shift my luggage. It was a warm and cozy room overlooking the Lake, just below the Naini Temple. I opened the windows of the room and got fascinated at the sight of mesmerizing beauty, just across the road. The crystal blue water of the Lake, kissed by the raindrops gently pouring from above right then, had just blown my mind. I made myself comfortable, with my belongings now settled in order, and then I took a shower. By that time, it started raining heavily. I dressed myself casually and walked out of the room towards the Lounge. As I had to wait for the weather to ameliorate, I ordered a cup of black tea and some light snacks. I was not that hungry even after traveling the whole day. I walked up to one corner of the Lounge and occupied a comfortable chair. I looked around and about the Lounge, picking up a magazine and going through it while waiting for my order to be served. It was a relaxing moment after the scorching heat that I had experienced the last few days. I was sitting there and wondering, how beautiful and amusing is the formation of The Creator, that, only at a distance of certain kilometers, changes in the entire atmosphere can happen so mystically.

Tea was now served, and as I enjoyed the food, I looked around and noticed that there was silence in the room and not many people were visible at the moment. There were few youngsters occupying the fancy-cushioned benches on the other side of the Lounge. Two young boys among them were playing the guitar while others in the group were silently listening and at times were hooting to encourage them. An elderly couple was also sitting by the fireplace in the other corner. To my left, A Lady in her thirties caught my attention. I noticed that she was not an Indian. She sat there all by herself with her legs stretched out, fully relaxed, and kept her eyes closed. She looked cool in a light pink bandhani kurta and plain pink dhoti set, with the floaters resting on the ground beside her. I observed her for a while. She was giving me a very pleasant vibe. I kept asking myself, "Should

I approach her and look toward a friendly cohesion?". At first, I hesitated wondering if she would like the move. After a while, I decided to give it a try at least. So, I walked up to her and wished her a pleasant evening.

I introduced myself… "Hi! I'm Sushmita, you can also call me Anna if you wish. We Indians have more than one name", and I smiled. "Can I have a seat?"

She looked up at me, and pulling back her legs together, she smiled and said, "Ah! Sure. Do join me please. By the way, I am Kyra".

I thanked her and took a seat opposite to her.

"Such a pleasant weather here. I'm already enjoying it, although I reached an hour back. How long have you been here? I asked.

"It's my third day today. Yes, everything about this place is enchanting and it's a treat to the mind-body-soul", she said.

Her words gave me a feeling of goosebumps for some time. No wonder, I was drawn towards her. By then, even the drizzles were gone. But it was wet all over and still cloudy. So, I asked her, "Would you like to join me for a walk? The breeze is cool and the smell of the wet soil has always been an alluring aroma".

"Yeah sure", came her instant response. "Got kinda bored sitting inside since morning".

"Oh! Had it been raining since morning?", I enquired.

"It started last night and is continuing", Kyra said, while putting on her floaters.

We both left our comfortable couches and walked out of the lobby. The climate outside gave me the feeling of 'Heaven on Earth'. The greenery around and the enthralling beauty that the Queen of the Hills exhibits is not at all surprising. It was so enchanting. We kept walking on the mall road and around the Lake. Kyra insisted that we sit by the lakeside and so I joined her.

"The water-body fascinates me always. I feel connected and very intuitively guided towards the beauty of Nature in its raw form". She expressed looking at me with a smile and I could see her eyes lit up. I too love Nature and can be all by myself for hours in its midst. I put a glance at Kyra. She looked beautiful in her baby pink dress which complimented her pale yellowish skin-tone, and copper-brown colored hair.

"Where do you belong to, Kyra?", I enquired

With a bright smile, she replied, "I belong to this Planet, this very Earth is my home."

I too chuckled at her humor.

"I am from North Carolina, my dear," she continued. "I am here on a holiday, a break I needed desperately".

"WOW! Are you traveling all by yourself?" I asked.

"Yes, this is one such time that I need to be all alone and I am enjoying my company." She answered

"You are so lucky Kyra. You come from a place on earth, which by itself is so beautiful. Such hypnotizing landscapes all over", I appreciated.

"Have you been there?", she questioned

"O no, I have just seen and enjoyed the beauty of your Country, in pictures so far," I replied with a smile. "Can you tell me a little more about your place in particular?".

"Yeah, why not? But you should visit the place, to bask in its beauty. I have been born and raised there, and so I grew up with the enchantment of the scenic beauty. Yet, the Country, my State, and the city I belong to, never fail to fascinate me again and again. Although, there is much more to add value to its beauty". She looked at a distance while speaking, as though she was trying to visualize.

"There is the famous Pisgah National Forest, in the western part of North Carolina. There are two-three more such sanctuaries. You will also like the Wright Brothers National Memorial Park. It's a truly lovely State with beautiful Seashores, Smokey Mountains, and several Parks. It is surrounded by several unbelievable natural beaches all around. You will have amazing experiences that this Tar Heel State has got to offer. You will just love the spectacular Sunrise and Sunset, snowclad Mountains in Winter, and so on". She looked at me with pride of honor and a smile in her eyes.

She took out her phone to show me the pictures saved in the gallery. I could only admire and keep saying "Wow!" each time. I kept gazing at the pictures of the - 469 Miles of the strikingly scenic Blue Ridge Parkway beauty. Oh! what a sight they all are. I simply fell in love with the land.

"I must visit someday for sure", I told her.

I looked around the Naini Lake now and noticed an old man preparing Tea at his tiny cozy shop, just at a distance.

"Would you like some Tea Kyra?". I asked and to which she gave a nod.

We decided to have a cup of tea each and we walked up to his shop. The old man had wrinkles all over his face and looked very cute. He maintained the shop very efficiently. It is clean and neat. I asked for two cups of Tea. Beside him, sitting on the wet ground was his wife. She placed some plastic rolls all over and sat on them. She was roasting some maize on a ' Chulah ' (sort of an iron oven that had been lit up by burning charcoals inside it). Although the lady is old, she looked enticing, in her colorful Indian dress, the 'lehenga-choli 'with a dupatta all around her, which she even pulled over her crown. She was wearing a lot of silver jewelry which looked traditional but worn out with time. I asked her for two of that juicy maize. She instantly roasted it for us and rubbed it with some black-salt and lemon juice. It tasted good and was a treat with piping hot black tea at this hour of the day when it started to be a bit cold due to the weather.

We carried the cups and moved towards a makeshift shed. There were a few huge logs cut into halves and placed there so that people could sit on them and rest for a while. It is nothing at all comfortable, yet a fun-filled activity for a change. We both sat down there and relished our eateries.

As we did so, I asked her –

"Have you flown down here, straight from your hometown? or are you on a planned trip to India? Have you visited more places before Nainital?"

To which Kyra's response was, "I had traveled to Delhi first. After three-four days, I took a road trip to Manali. Oh, what a breathtaking place it is. I love the Beas River that flows all through nature and into the township. I had a joyful experience and enjoyed my stay at Manali for more than a week, and now am here. I am loving the peace and serenity of these beautiful hill stations in India. Manali days were so calm and enchanting for me. I needed the tranquility, Anna, that I was missing back at home".

She paused for a while and said, "I had been going through a nerve-wracking phase in my life past four to five years now. I didn't know how to tackle, or should I say handle the shattered pieces of the various aspects of my life. I was looking for every means and every help that I could gather, to manage the sanity I needed desperately, but nothing seemed to work. So, at that time the decision of getting away from the regular struggle that I had to face, day in and day out, and running into the lap of Nature to look for solace, did help to bring some changes in my life. And since then, every six months interval, I invariably plan to travel all around. I make it a choice that I mostly travel to the Hills and Mountains".

There was a bit of silence now.

I then said, "Yeah, I do get it. Every other person in this World, is going through some problem or other in life".

She nodded.

I continued speaking… "Society has changed to a great extent by the norms, and altered the lifestyle so much so that, at times, it becomes difficult to understand what we are supposed to do".

"Well, that's some issue for sure. But when I speak of my problem, I mean it to be - esoteric". She added with a giggle.

I was looking at her and noticed that each time she smiles, her eyes lit up and enhances her beauty even more. The dimples in her cheeks become prominent, and her eyes expressive and intense.

"Esoteric, Wow! Interesting!! Would you mind putting some light on it", I requested and noticed a positive sign from her. "Hey, I understand that you are mentioning some higher level of personal experience, but just imagine …if you share, you will guide me towards something important for myself and others, and help a few of us to elevate. Isn't it?"

She looked at me and I winked back at her with a smile. She burst out in laughter.

"Hmm… I don't know why am I even unearthing personal experiences before you, but I am liking it. It's almost two years or more, that I never chose to look back at my past, or even speak about it to anyone else. Well today as I decide to do, I feel that it must have reasons and some deeper meaning too. Ok, let's take it as a sign from the higher self", she said.

I looked at her and asked, "Kyra… will you allow me to jot down points that I feel are important for me.? I mean, as you speak and share your experiences, I wish to note down certain things that draw my attention. These might later on help me and others as we try to walk a path similar to yours. I am an aspiring writer Kyra, and if you will, I would like to share your opinion someday through my work and I am sure it will contribute to the greater good of humanity."

She looked at me a little surprised and said, "Hey, glad to know about you, and although I can't see if this will help, I'm okay with it. I have no objection if you wish to write"

I was excited by then. I almost rushed her up to finish her work in the market, if she had any. So that, we could walk back to the Hotel and I could listen to her story, as she discloses her mystical journey. She expressed her desire to collect some local food items for dinner later. We looked all around and found a street where the local ladies were selling cooked food, some delicacies of their community. Kyra loved the look of the preparation and decided to pack some for herself. I was surprised to see her buying vegetarian dishes. When I enquired, she said that she no longer took non-veg items or alcohol and wine. I liked this about her as I too had turned a vegetarian sometime back. Together we walked back to the Hotel. The city had come to life now. All places and shops were lit up and people thronged into the street. Although the darkness of the night fell all over the place, it added up awe to the esteemed charm and enthralling beauty. It took us less than half-hour to reach our Hotel and I immediately rushed to my room to collect my pen and notepad. Kyra was waiting for me, in her room. As I knocked on her door, I could hear the unique sound of Sitar. I got curious… was she playing the music? Kyra opened the door and as I stepped in, the aroma of fresh coffee was lingering all over the room. I noticed that the music was playing on her iPod.

"I am brewing some coffee for us. I suppose you like it, don't you?", she asked."

"Oh yeah, I wouldn't mind some right now, although I am not so fond of the beverage. I prefer tea more," I told her.

I looked around and sat on the sofa that was placed near the windows overlooking the garden area of the Hotel. It is a beautiful site, nicely maintained all over with lights and potted plants here and there beside the natural plantations. People were pacing up and down the lawn, while children were playing around. I looked up at the sky and the waning moon just beamed at me. The stars were sparkling too. A rare site to see, in other big cities because of the pollution. Kyra came over with the coffee and placed it on the side table that was lying there. I picked a cup and as I took a sip, I asked her, "So you love Sitar, hmm! Do you even play?", to which she replied…

"O no, I only love listening a lot, I even enjoy the classical work of the Indian Maestro, Ravi Shankar at times. It helps me keep my calm".

"Kyra, what I have assumed so far by listening to you, I feel you have experienced spirituality to its highest order, is that so?" I inquired, "Well, I'm really curious about all that happened during the process. I have no such knowledge yet, though I did hear a few people discussing the matter and am excited. As I meet you today and am understanding that you are in the same boat, I feel it thrilling to visit the pathway through your experience."

She looked at me and said quite seriously, "It only sounds gracious and interesting dear, but you should know that you have to pay a heavy price too. Although you gain a lot of internal happiness but remember, it's not a pleasant journey at all" She suddenly looked pale.

"What is spiritual awakening?", she asked almost to herself and continued. "To each, it's his-her own story and experience. For me, it's a process of undergoing seasonal teachings of life. Just as we experience the major four seasons of Nature, life too teaches us the experiences of our personal four seasons…, similar to Spring, Summer, Autumn, and Winter, which comes as a cycle of upheaval lessons for us, with a mixture of joy and happiness time to time. These are Lessons that were meant to teach us all that we need to know and master, to be free from the web of illusion. These lessons help us on our Soul growth and advance us towards the path of self-realization, Divine Wisdom, and also the realization of Oneness"

"Interesting, please carry on", is all I could say.

I preferred to only listen to her, on all that she had to say. So, I decided to maintain total silence from then on.

Kyra took a few more sips of her coffee silently. The sitar music kept on playing in the background, creating an atmosphere of peace and tranquility. She was constantly gazing at the beauty outside her room.

"It has been five years now", Kyra spoke up suddenly. "Life started to take me out on a super-ride, all through the uncertainty and the unknown." She sighed deeply and continued. "I had always been an introvert. I would mostly love to keep to myself. Sometimes, when my mother would enquire why I hardly spoke, I had no definite answer to that. All I understood was, I enjoyed my own company more. I love to read and so any book that caught my interest would be my company. I am not fascinated by any particular genre of writing, nor do I have a favorite Author. I just love to read good stuff. I am thoroughly a creative person and so, music, the art of any form, gardening, painting, etc. facinates me and I can keep myself busy with such activities the whole day long if I am free from academic pursuits. I also enjoy most of my alone time walking by the sea-shore. I can remain sitting there, and daydream of becoming an interior designer, or designing clothes for the fashionistas. I love this sort of creative idea. It's enthralling." She took a deep breath and continued…

"I have limited friends, not because I don't enjoy their company, but because I would always be looking forward to the time when I could be back home. The only thing I love to do wholeheartedly is, visit the auditoriums whenever some good Plays were enacted by well-known dramatists and actors. I also love going to the concerts now and then. I prefer and enjoy classical art-forms more. Life according to me, was all good. I hardly had a complaint about anything, other than my disability to travel all around the world. I could not manage enough money to do so. I was nineteen years and had no steady relationship yet. Of course, I had a few short-time in-and-out connections, but nothing interesting and so I never thought of continuing them. I was never interested in taking any sort of relationship to a serious level without being relatively sure. I had no interest in flings and I always knew that I had to have as a partner someone loyal, in whom I am to invest emotionally. Most of the time, I spend reading in the library of my university or the Canteen, all by myself, because my friends had other plans with their mates. Hence, I gradually mastered the skill of a Hermit".

Kyra giggled this time and continued. "Even At home, as I am the only child, I would keep to myself mostly. A certain period would be dedicated to my mother, as I love her company. Helping her in the kitchen and with other household chores made our bond strong. But mostly, it is me and my art and craft equipment and music. Those had become my all-time favorite associates. In the evenings, I often do go for a walk by the beach as my home is just overlooking the Sea. Early morning and at night whenever I keep awake, I can hear the splashing sound of the waves, hitting the shore. It's my favorite place to be, whenever I feel lonely. Although I do have a few of my friends who live close by, I can hardly think of anyone with whom I can share my deepest thoughts. I am not a party animal and I don't even socialize much. Going to Church every Sunday is also not a mandatory activity for me. Rather I prefer decorating the house and arranging the Altar just as the way I feel connected and remain close to God in the privacy of my home. Life was somewhat pleasant for me and my family, at least this is what I can say as I look back today. We were all happy together. My parents took good care of me, provided a good education, and also helped me to be self-sufficient. We were and still are, three individuals of different identities yet always ready to be there for each other without hesitation and expectations. My father owned a grocery shop which had been our strength, our source of good business always. My mother often helped him throughout the day and together they earned well. The late evenings had always been moments of merriment at home. My parents made it a definite ritual to prepare dinner together unless my father had some business work to deal with. So, cooking food and being in each-other's company, having a drink or two, and dancing to the tunes of good music, were a constant site at my home. My grandparents were also living in the same city but at a distance and so, Sunday would be special. Either we were visiting them or they would come over to spend the night with us. It was a joyful moment for all, and we would end up retiring to bed with content-full hearts, and gratitude towards God for all His blessings. This had been our reality up to my 20th birthday."

Kyra paused for some time. She picked up her water bottle and took a sip. She looked at me and as she spoke again, she sounded a little hurt, "Anna, life took a sudden change from here and we had never anticipated it. Suddenly there seemed to be the shadow of a huge grey cloud upon us. One night, someone or maybe more people broke into my father's store and left us with heavy losses. Several items were damaged and many things were taken away, leaving the store almost empty of the stock and in a devastated condition. We could not trace the burglars ever. Since then, everything seemed to fall apart. At first, my father tried to figure out how to mend the splinters to get back into the previous situation. He tried for months together but every effort seemingly failed. Slowly, he lost all hope and started to panic. Friends and family tried to boost him up with moral support but saw zero results. He lost his willpower and gradually sank into depression. He started drinking a lot and as a result, my parents ultimately ended up in fights and conflicts. I didn't know how to help. I couldn't keep watching my father suddenly grow old and his health deteriorating each day. It hurt me to notice my mother keep crying silently almost every night. A bad omen seemed to fall upon the family. She kept visiting some primary schools and other workplaces in search of a job but in vain. She returned home like a lost warrior every single day. All of a sudden, the lively home turned out to be a pathetic place to live in. Each of us was dealing with our demons and somehow coping with days that were coming as they may. Had we any choice otherwise? No dear, not at the moment. We no longer felt hungry or had the desire to eat and cook. Life had become mechanical. Each day we woke up with new hope and set out on new paths to succeed in dreamt endeavors but came back frustrated and lost.

Several truths were also brought to light for us, during this period. Despite extending help to people earlier, my father could not find anyone to help him in return at times of our dismay. One or two of his friends did offer financial help but it wasn't sufficient to establish the strong foundation of the business, that had towered down badly. I too searched for part-time jobs but people who seemed to be convinced of my ability somehow didn't take me seriously. I was turned down with a polite note, "We'll get back to you soon", which of course never happened. This was the worst chilly winter phase of our life, although it was the July-August month. Every day seemed like a new struggle which ended up in sleepless nights that nevertheless brought us into hopeless situations. One night, as I couldn't sleep at all, I got down from my bed and walked up to the kitchen for some water. I filled a glass of water and as I took some sips, my eyes wandered towards the Altar and I walked up to that one sacred corner of the Portico. It is adjacent to the kitchen. I lit the candle that was placed there before the idol of Mother Mary and Lord Jesus and also a few Angel statues that are my favorites. It was past midnight. I sat before them with folded hands and fell on my knees and started questioning, as to what mistake on our part led us to this fate. That particular night for a while, I continuously prayed and repeatedly asked for their help and requested them to show light and clarity on our situation. There were moments when I got mad at them and broke down into tears, and yet again, I felt relaxed and centered after a while. I repeatedly kept asking my Angels to show me signs, if they were connected to me at that moment. I sat there in silence for another hour and suddenly, I noticed that outside the window pane, the shadow of some birds could be seen. They were circling the house and were mobbing. I walked up to the window to see if it is real or if it was only an illusion. As I lifted the curtain I saw two birds, one - a barn owl, and the other a Raven. They were chasing each other and whenever they came into proximity, they made physical contact and hit each other hard. I partially lifted the corner of the curtain and kept watching, as I didn't want to distract them. I kept praying out of fear, while they kept hitting each other for some time until one seemed to win the battle and so they left. The fear was about an uncertain omen that the presence of these birds seems to interpret at the moment".

Saying so, she paused for a while as if to recollect the event. She was looking intensely at a distance outside and continued,

"I don't know when I had fallen asleep that night, but I woke up relaxed and light-hearted. I woke up a bit late the next morning. The whole house was silent and I realized that I was the only person at home. My parents must have left early today on their mission and so no one woke me up. I made a cup of Coffee for myself when I noticed a few pancakes, covered with a glass lid that rested by the cooktop. My mother must have made them before leaving. I was thankful to her for I felt a little hungry by then. I sat on a bench on the verandah adjacent to our kitchen and was trying to figure out all that I had visualized the previous night. It must be some signs for me from my Angels is what I kept thinking, when, a beautiful yellow color butterfly came flying towards the potted plants and then kept circling me. I picked up my phone and looked for a significant meaning and it said 'change'. I knew deep down in my gut, that some changes would come in our situation with time. I also strangely felt a sense of strong energetic protection out of the blue. Now whether the changes are for good or bad, is for me to wait and watch", She said with a faint smile on her face.

I was still curious and so kept waiting for her to continue. She refilled her cup with coffee and said… "few days passed by in the same manner. We all kept trying for means of earning. One evening, Dad came home with happy news. He said that an old friend came forward to help him financially and joined his business as a partner. Although this was not what he was expecting, anything that came toward us then to partially end our trouble is a silver lining in disguise. We all were feeling grateful that our winter would now somehow come to an end. We were ready to welcome the colors of 'Spring' although with a little discomfort through the transition, yet we were happy. It had been tough though to share with someone all that was Ours earlier. My mother was not comfortable with the idea but there was no other choice. Hence emotional conflicts between my parents continued. They started finding indifferences in almost everything which made the environment at home still tumultuous and heavy at times. I could understand their emotions and knew that they were both going through a rough time, but what happens between adults in a relationship, and that too behind closed doors, is not what anybody else can judge. All one can do is seek the peace that will come eventually. At least that's what we were hoping for.

Meanwhile, my connection with my Angels grew stronger each day and most of the time, I found myself sitting before my Altar in silence. This gave me mental support at least. By then, I had also joined a Cafe during the evening shift after my UNI classes. Although I was not paid truly well, it helped me to pay my fees and buy my books. Things started looking good for some time until my mother started falling ill. She was diagnosed with a lung problem that gave her terrible pain and difficulty in breathing. Now here came the biggest challenge for us. Visit to the doctors and hospitalization at times, were demanding huge expenses. My father at first took it lightly, but how long? He started complaining about the expenditure that had become an extra burden now. My mother took his reactions personally and developed emotional pain too. Relation between them grew denser and they started drifting apart. I helplessly watched my mother sulk and silently sink into the persistent feeling of sadness. It had become a frustrating situation for me and I could do nothing much. A few days started turning into Prolonged waits and every single day seemed to fall heavy on us. I kept wondering when the circumstance will change and things will start coming together. There didn't seem any other way except keeping faith and hope in the Almighty", She sighed.

"Was there no other way to get help? Did you consult any Astrologer?" I asked.

"No, I don't believe in astrology much. Yes, the planetary positions do affect our life, but I don't think any Astrologer can help in changing our circumstances unless we decide to change them by ourselves. Yes, it does take time, but gradually we'll see the change of positivity is what I always believed and this trust grew stronger with time." She replied.

"And how do we do that?", I enquired.

"Well, all that I understood, during this difficult phase of my life is, to strengthen our faith in the Supreme power. I had a strong feeling since my childhood that there is some energy - force mightier than all, and could bend us just the way we need to and alter our situation. I now hardly visit any Church. Instead, I spend more time working on my inner strength and focus on developing a strong connection with the Universe. This is when I heard a lot about spiritualism from friends and they even suggested I follow motivational speakers. I started reading some books that were on the subject matter, to understand the spiritual bend in our life. Doing so, I understood that it does help to bring us into awareness, but no one can help me or my family in this situation with advice alone. Something needs to be done by ourselves to improve our situation and it's around this time that the concept of ' law of attraction ' came through strongly for me. I surfed the Net to explore every detail that was available in connection to these manifestations. I earlier did not know these techniques and the more I looked into it, the more confused I was. I had followed every idea and every suggestion that people advised but nothing seemed to work. I eventually gave up on everything and followed my heart's calling", She said.

"Did you find solace after all that you did, to conclude your situation?", I asked.

"Yes, dear. But I want to make it clear to you that it didn't happen overnight. Challenges came our way now and then and some were nerve-wracking. At times, I lost hope but my Angels kept me going with their full support and helped me strengthen my faith. With time, I must say, we did find peace, happiness, and revival of our lost situation, just the way we deserve. Yes, we did complete our cycle of the four seasons and brought an end to our suffering of this difficult phase in life. But it's not the end. Now, we or I may say, especially I, am prepared to take a journey ahead that might put me in such situations again but I am confident to overcome it each time.", having said that, she completed her story for this once, as it was past her dinner time. I took her consent for seeking help whenever I need and she readily agreed. We exchanged our Email ID and She showed eagerness to look forward to meeting each other again. I came to my room and kept recollecting whatever she had said and although not everything about her situation was clear to me, I felt a connection somewhere. I knew I would have to give serious thought to some matters, as I could see myself in similar situations. Although I understood that Kyra had not put out everything of her life that would be of help to me, yet, whatever I could gather had been my learning. Some similarities are always there and her experience would help me as guidance in my life path. I stayed there for another day, and when we met the next morning, we had a fun time together and did some not-so-necessary shopping. She shared a few more troublesome moments of her struggle and I knew I was learning a lot. I understood that these teachings would be of help to me shortly and I felt grateful to have met her. I thanked the Almighty for this fated meeting. I believe this to be fated because, I suddenly came upon someone unknown, who had been talking to me for hours now, on a subject I knew was a necessity for me too. I felt relaxed and satisfied with the connection we just built together and this definitely must have been my soul's craving.

The next few days, I traveled to nearby places and after about a week, I flew back home but this time with a more mature mindset. My curiosity about life and its various colors kept increasing as I too had been going through a lot of mixed emotions which sometimes perplexed me hugely. After the tour when I entered the placid atmosphere of my home, I sensed an emptiness for the first time. I had always been comfortable on my own and preferred it mostly that way. Yet, this time, the hollowness within me screamed out loud.

Suddenly, out of no-where I felt the urge to know myself… who am I? Why am I here? What is my purpose? Yes, there was now a lot of question in my mind and I have reasons for it. What is it that I am missing? My childhood had been pleasant no doubt, although if I look back today, it won't be called a normal one. According to me, I had the best of everything as I grew up. The education provided was perfect, I had opportunities to pursue other curricular activities, enjoyed merriment, and had the freedom of movement, despite being a girl child. So, what is it that keeps me troubled? I realized that sometimes, my mind would not be at peace and I knew I need to address this restless state. Time passed by and I was still looking for the answer I so desperately need to know.

* * * * *

THE VOID

Come *December* 2019, And…

The surprise news of a new Virus spread all over the world. "Outbreak of Covid-19 began in Wuhan, China" … was the headline all over the Newspapers, Television, and Social-Media. At first, it was only a matter of concern for China due to their prudent negligence, as per concerted opinion. People all over our country and around the world were looking at China to be faulty and were discussing the matter with disgust. Initially, not only India but it was taken lightly by other Countries too. People were generally happy that they now got a reason to take a break from the mundane life, happily staying at home availing some free time to share with family. Gradually situation started changing for a lot of people. The initial days of the pleasant stay at home had now started to become a punishment. Women found it difficult the most, as they had to dedicate some extra time in the kitchen now, and those who are into jobs had the office-work pressure too. Dealing with troublesome and toxic relationships, mischievous children, and nagging in-laws are some additional factors of the distasteful daily dosage of life, (all of these in some cases only) made situations difficult for many. Peace and harmony were lost. News of Corona-Virus becoming the brutal truth to bring havoc in people's lives all over the world, created panic in every household. People were losing their near and dear ones and hence were becoming emotionally trapped within their victim minds.

Where was I being affected by all of this?

The news was a hindrance for me too. Although my part of India experienced the effect of the virus much later. I was living in North-East India at that time. There were no cases initially, but a fear of being exposed and affected by the virus was always there. My husband being a Banker, had to go to the office daily. So, remaining at home would not keep me safe. This is a practical thought I had and I was prepared for anything destined. My trouble was not us, but my son who had been abroad then. He was a medical student out there for his studies and how he would manage to keep himself protected, was my concern. I kept praying day and night, but would prayer alone help? I am sure, those who lost their lives did pray till the last minute. But honestly, was the virus our only concern? If so, people should have been happy, once the virus was over. Everyone should have felt relieved, to find themselves safe and healthy and feel blessed with full family around. Yet, this was not what happened. Those who became fortunate enough to survive didn't see the full blessing in their situation. Getting the opportunity for a short period, they must have considered themselves to be lucky but then, the regular drama of several painful and toxic situations started tapping into most people's life.

Well, I am not here to judge anybody's life and its shortcomings. I am emphasizing this matter, only because I am being called by my inner guidance, (that which is beyond our control). I had been asked to share my personal story, my journey on a path of inner knowing… How and what I have been through, and what I did, to come out of all the dark situations in my life so far. I was repeatedly told (intuitively) that, my experience might be of help to many who are going through similar situations. And this is what I am trying my best to do here. I am now taking the help of my pen to share all possible measures that I took, to come out of… mental, emotional, psychological, physical, and spiritual pain. Here, I am going to exempt the experience of spiritual upliftment, mostly because this is not something that many might understand, as, not everyone is ready for the shake-up of conscious awakening yet.

The void in my life unfolded majorly due to the spiritual awakening. What I have had to experience, is because of the nudge and preparation that the awakening did bring in for me, to transform my life massively. A period of stillness shook me to the core, to ultimately realize the deep essence of nothingness and travel through the comprehension of oneness. A huge disclaimer as "alert" is what I am putting here for my readers now… "Please read the content with an open mind. Understand the situations without any judgment, and take to follow any of the steps that you fancy, without any expectation that it will help a hundred percent. Not everyone will be having the same problems and so take only those issues to judgment and concern, which resonates with you, and then, try to apply the shared measures to better your life. If it works, you will henceforth be having a blessed life."

A few months before the virus struck out, I started experiencing several issues in life that disturbed me mentally and emotionally for quite some time. I couldn't understand where it was coming from and why such issues were purging at this time of life when there was nothing around to bother me. I was almost free from responsibilities as my only child had been living far away from us. Being the two of us now at home and as my husband focused on his job alone, there was nothing to burden me. I always had the freedom to move around at my will wherever I wished to. So, what could be the problem? Now... If I wish to share emotions and their after-effects that kept flowing through my life, I'll need to mention, to an extent, a bit about my journey so far. And here it goes...

Not so unusual, yet unfortunately, I am a child born into a middle-class family in the 70s but never grew up with them. In my infancy, many unforeseen episodes of unwanted situations took place that resulted in a separation between me and my bio family at the earliest part of my life. We were into the joint family concept and nine other children were growing up together, which resulted in a chaotic situation for all the parents and the grandparents. Several unavoidable circumstances (such as grandparents falling sick, family members meeting with major accidents, another childbirth, etc.) led my family of fifteen members constantly living together, to take the ultimate decision of handing over the responsibility of my upbringing to very close family friends at the age of one. It's not that I was away from their sight but never had been considerably cared for by them since then. Time and again I kept visiting and meeting them, yet never had been an integral part of the family. The decisions of the family always existed in every external matter of my reality but never had been cohesive, to engrave any impression in my sense of belonging. This of course has been in the long run, a boon in disguise for me and I realized this only with time. With all due respect to both my families, paying equal gratitude to them, I convey that I still love my second family a little more. Hey, don't judge me. I grew up there with the utmost care, affection, and love, and so I truly desire to pay my homage to them with such honor. They have taken every step and means to provide the best life for me till I decided to marry.

After marriage, it has always been the three of us as a family... me, my husband, and my son, although initially, I had to live with my in-laws for some time. This period, four years approximately, was of course a mixed baggage of joy, misery, liking and disliking, just as any other joint-family in India gets to experience. Being the youngest in all forms and shapes to every relation I got introduced to, I had to keep hold of my strong disliking, within me, as, we younger ones are always expected to be obedient and disciplined. This is so casually practiced as prudence in Indian society at all times. It is a way to show respect to the elders. Such was my life for a long time since then. My child came into my life and became an important part only after three years of my marriage. It should have been an enjoyable time for us but the irony was, I repeatedly kept falling sick at intervals and this continued from childbirth till the recent past. I was troubled by frequent rush-up to the hospitals, followed by blood tests and unnecessary medications that kept changing now and then. With me, the funny thing that happened was, my reports of blood tests were always normal. The doctors would still find out a cause and diagnose something or the other because they had to. Hence, the medicines never worked. When my son turned eight years old, an unknown person from a nearby locality where I lived and whom I met accidentally, said that I was under the influence of dark-magic spells. Now this was a new concept for me. I heard a lot about it but never expected this to happen to me. I was given all sorts of proof to confirm the ill effect that caused ill health. I found it quite fascinating and eagerly followed whatever advised, to tarnish its effect, although in vain. I started reading on this matter to reach its depth.

During this phase, my physical body experienced several types of ailments which were most common in nature, yet, some were so unnatural and intense that it made me land in the hospital as an outpatient sometimes. But nothing was ever clinically detected to be called a serious illness. Only, we were spending money unnecessarily without any positive result to be seen. Not failing to mention here that I had taken up the help of some sort of social practices too, to get rid of my problems. These practices did work but issues were relapsing no doubt. Well, many of you might be wondering what all issues did I suffer due to the spells. Yet again many of you won't even believe that such things might be the cause or such things ever exists. Since I took to share, so let me anyway mention a few experiences that I had been through. When my son was only four months old, one morning I woke up with my entire body swollen up. I could not open my eyes. Out of the blue, I found myself with a wardrobe full of clothes that were no longer fitting me. It is still like a dream to me. Suddenly one fine morning I could not walk properly, and could not understand why I started bloating. I could not breastfeed my child more than twice throughout the day. I had to start baby food even at the late hours of the night when he would cry in hunger. I tried all means to get out of the hexes or curses, whatever it had been but failed. This was only the beginning. One night after dinner I could not sleep as I had been continuously running to the loo and after twenty-seven times of rushing to and from, I lost my sense and fell unconscious at the break of dawn. Gradually, I developed anger issues that affected me more internally, because I was not expressing it. Some incidents bothered me but my family would address it to be normal. I would find grains of rice between the mattresses that are covered with vermillion and never understand how they appeared there but my husband overlooked them. I refrained from sharing anything that was damaging my psyche. I couldn't sleep peacefully throughout the night as I would frequently experience some unseen energy trying to press me on the chest and not letting me breathe. I could never express my feelings without being judged and so I always chose to remain silent on such matters. I had been an empath all my life and hence, a compromiser in all situations. I could understand that everyone was taking advantage of my compassion but could do nothing about it. I would be hurt for a while, cry out to release the grievances, and then give up on the issue because I knew that eventually I would get cornered. Being the emotional victim, all that I did was, a little injustice to my child because I could not be at times available physically to attend to his needs. At times I even unwillingly and unknowingly hurt the innocent child's psyche by venting my suppression on an innocent kid.

Physical suffering and inability to remain active all time had become the major cause of bitter indignation. Altogether, everything affected our day-to-day life activities and happiness including indifferences in opinion sometimes. All of that led to affecting the home situation in bitter-sour ways intermittently. Yet, no matter what, we did manage to bring harmony at the end of the day and this is what we were looking up to and what we truly wanted. So, life went on. The peaceful accord particularly helped me maintain my sanity despite all physical agonies. Hence there was a maintained balance. My husband being the ever-grateful one for his job and dedicated towards his work, kept himself busy with office activities. As such, he mostly ignored issues related to the home front and kept himself busy and away from chaos. His silence and disassociation played a dual role. On one side it frustrated me to see his disengagement, but on the other hand, his silence is what I was looking for, perhaps because it served me as the ointment needed to cure my emotional wound. This is what I honestly felt in my later recovery days. But not everybody will understand or accept the theory. Life went on in this manner until my son's board exams. He is a sharp child and did extremely well in academics despite the ill effects of spells cast on us. This made him and his father believe that he would manage on his own to continue his study in some other city. Mostly, children these days wish to go out for their education and so did he. I, for instance, was against this decision and kept requesting not to go with the plan, but they both ignored my suggestion. I was the one working up constantly on the psychic attacks that were sent toward us. I knew that once he sets out of the house, it would be difficult for me to manage control of the so-called bewitchment intended on us, that too at two different places far from each other. My people mocked the sort of illiterate sense of my belief and uncanny behavior. Finally, after several efforts, I had to call it a day on my suggestion and started preparing for his forward march. My son joined College away from us, in due course.

The first time out of home, the absence troubled us both…mother and son. He was trying his best to present himself as a mature child but failed drastically when comes to emotion. I too thought that I would manage quite well but coping with emptiness both externally and internally took a toll on my health. By his final year, I fell sick with Herpes zoster syndrome that added up to periodical traumatic episodes and this ruined the entire planning of our life. My son could not ignore seeing me in pain and hence suffered emotionally which resulted in a setback in his academic performance for the first time. He was unable to perform as expected and this disturbed us all mentally. Meanwhile, I too had been going through Hell with the painful experience of Herpes. Unbearable Physical pain with a combination of royal ignorance of reasoning from close people… relatives and friends, and even my husband, was commendable. I was bedridden but nobody had bothered to call and enquire about my health. I had a regular tendency of calling up near and dear ones to know their whereabouts. But now that my frequent calls were almost nil, nobody seemed to notice the silence. I do admit that I was taken care of by my husband but only till the blisters could be seen externally. After the recovery of the topical rashes caused by the shingles, he could not fathom the reason why I still preferred to remain in bed. I could not convince him that I was having serious complications internally. The fact that my people were beyond compassion and understanding, as to what it must be like to go through such tumultuous conditions, was disturbing my spirit from the core. Realizing that I was going through a depressing state, and suffering physically and emotionally, my son became anxious and started to feel low in silence. Neither of us got to notice this. But situations did militate his anima so much so that, eight months before his final exams he became stressed and suddenly caught the dengue fever. I had to shift with him, ignoring the bodily discomfort that I had been trying to overcome post Herpes and Neuropathic disorders. I discounted my needs because my son had been my priority always. I needed to be there, by his side during his troublesome period. He was trying to cope with the classes that he had missed for days due to ill health and also prepare for the boards. Of-course he had been expected by all of us to be prepared for the NEET exams as well, that would soon follow. So, the pressure built up. Little did I realize that juggling between two modes of education, a normal science course for the board and the coaching pattern for competitive exams, was not an easy task. That too when a child misses more than twenty classes physically due to dengue. I too did suffer, to maintain a good diet for him and me both. In an unknown city, managing everything all by myself despite ill-health, had been difficult but every engagement paid off because I had once again got to enjoy a period of childlike freedom, that I got to relive in his Hostel for a while.

During this phase, I got the opportunity to meet several other mothers who were residing in the same hostel to support their children. Provisions for the parents to reside there separately were arranged by the Hostel authorities. I made some good friends then, who continue to be in the circle even now. Meanwhile, time heals anything and everything is what had always been prevailing famously in our belief system, and I too took this saying considerably at its true value. By the coming year, I felt I was done with the distorted memories of painful events. Peaceful time also seemed to start flowing in simultaneously, at least I thought so. But then came the time when my child couldn't perform as expected from him overall, through the 12th Board exam. We felt we have now entered into a nerve-wracking situation as this was a crucial period for him. We were typically expecting the 95% result that most parents of intelligent children do. Being devastated, we thought that life had to be decided on that one performance factor and so we behaved hyper. We, as parents, did hurt him and his sentiment by putting the burden and guilt of irresponsibility on his shoulder and of course created a major blunder. We probably told him many times, that he should have taken measures to put his full effort into the seriousness of his studies. Little did we realize, that as circumstances were so against him, he could have ended up failing to perform at all. But he successfully managed to beg decent result. I take the responsibility now, and state that, it was and still is negligence on our part, we as parents, our crude perception, and our ignorance, which we failed to notice at that given time. Having said that, I wish to point out here for parents to ponder, on my personal opinion… "Is it necessary for us to dream on behalf of our children and impose that desire on them, to be fulfilled for us? Could we do anything in life as we had expected, for ourselves? Could we satisfy our expectations in life? I am sure, the answer is no for most of us. Then Why can't we allow them to grow as individuals who have dreams to fulfill and lead a wonderful life? Well, we get to learn only from our mistakes, although many fail to do even that".

Considering our helpless state then, we tried every means to get him into higher educational fields, and destiny pulled him towards medical study in UKRAINE. Simultaneously, at the same time, he had been called in JIPMER too, but the father-son duo preferred the foreign degree because they felt that a medical degree from abroad would be largely beneficial. Also, my son always had a longing to live abroad for his studies and now he had the chance. Once again, not so willing to the decision, I still gave my concern because it would be unnecessary to try otherwise. And he traveled in the midyear of 2018. After that, a year passed by smoothly on the home front, although physically I still had been undergoing the recovery process from autoimmune diseases now. Feeling lonely, all alone throughout the day, I enrolled myself in EFLU, affiliated with NEHU, the Meghalaya University, to study the German language. It had been an experience of a kind to be in a class of students who were half my age. But I enjoyed being with them and they too welcomed me with love. But the happiness didn't last long. Suddenly, not for us alone, but due to the Virus, the entire world fell prey to the wrath of devastation. The havoc that Covid-19 had shown, was perhaps created by the mistakes that humanity was responsible for. Movement all around had become stagnant. I somehow completed my first-year course online. Everywhere and almost every department of education or Official service, exempting the emergency ones, had started working online. That's when, many people had gone through the mental trauma of losing their jobs, suffered physically because of the virus, and several unfortunate ones lost their life. It had been a nightmare for all. But life had to go on regardless of losses. People tried to cope with whatever situation they were in. For some, it was even merriment and they are fortunate, I must say. No matter what, people were craving for the return of normalcy. My son could not come home for more than a year. The situation out there was also not pleasant. No regular classes were taken and hence no practical experience was rendered for the upcoming doctors. He started losing interest in the course.

Now, came a new phase of regular tension for us at home. He started expressing his will to discontinue his studies there, while his father was trying to convince him to somehow complete the course. And as if this was not enough for me to tackle, destiny dropped into my lap the adverse effect of a phase of the "Spiritual Awakening series". This is a time when people cross the pool of cleansing and release the life of Riley, unwillingly. Many choose to walk the path of discomfort to ultimately receive the goodness of a Divinely rich life, while a few are "The Chosen Ones".

I entered this phase without any knowledge of how to navigate through it. It was a time when without reason, I kept purging out all the unnecessary emotions that were perhaps stored deep within my subconscious mind. I kept finding fault with every relationship I have in life. The me, who earlier felt blessed about my childhood, was suddenly feeling abandoned. For the first time, I realized that the thought of being sent out of home at the age of one year had suddenly not gone well with me. Several wrong expressions, misbehavior, and ignorance from both sides of the family partially, have contributed to the cause when I lost my ego control and held out forward, the most difficult question for my family. The question of… WHY ME? This action of mine made them uncomfortable and they avoided me thinking it would be only a matter of a passing time and I would be in a normal state soon. But at the age of fifty-plus, when this is the divine timing of awakening to 'my truth ', why on earth would I stop questioning? I was being energetically shaken up to clear the dark spaces that I had built, in all the chambers of my mind about every aspect of my life. Most of the turmoil was happening without my asking for it, but nobody agreed, and neither did they believe me.

* * * *

THE FOUR SEASONS

I don't know how many of you will even register with its kind, "The Awakening", but those who do will understand the discomfort, the pain, and the chivalry one faces while treading the most valuable and sacred path. Life, as a result, gave me pleasure as well as nightmares during my journey through the 'Dark Night of the Soul'. I at that moment, remembered Kyra and realized what she had meant when she shared phases of her experience through several seasons. I for that matter, recall my journey from The Winter.

I will refrain from sharing the deep undergoing of my experiences spiritually, as, not all will be on the same page to understand its depth. Those who are fortunately experiencing their sacred soul journey at this time will find similarities and can grab whatever they can gather as tools here. And those who are not even aware of the term 'spiritual awakening' might still find some connection with your lifestyle as you go through the pages. If you do, your help to an extent is available through the reading. Take all that resonates with each one of you, and leave what does not. I have been called (spiritually) to share my experiences; if this benefits my readers, it would mean a lot to me. I wish to start with my winter season because the trail of my story goes in that order.

I have been continuously wandering through several hardships since childhood (mostly emotional), and now I understand that all of it was connected to the lessons I had to undertake to prepare for the "Awakening". But as for all my readers, this is not the case, I am emphasizing general conditions and situations that almost everyone goes through in their life. Although these simple issues have also been a part of my spiritual lessons. Now, for those who feel that you never had any of the said experiences, well, you are the blessed ones and so, be grateful to Almighty for that.

* * * * *

THE WINTER

During the Corona-Virus phase, in my part of the Country, Shillong-Meghalaya, (we lived there at that time due to my husband's posting), reality due to the breakout of the virus came to us much later. Although there was hardly any positive case initially, I was unable to move out of the house. Movement there was restricted for all and if disobeyed, people would be fined heavily. My husband's duty fell under emergency service, so he would be at his office by Ten O'clock sharp. I had by then completed my course on Language study and was at home all by myself. The loneliness had started bothering me without my knowledge. I had no one to communicate with as everyone at that period was in a panic with the circumstance, and hence fear for their safety became a conscious after-effect. Slowly, the boredom resulted in a state of mind which led me to lament my condition and I gradually would break down into tears. Meanwhile, to add up to the misery, a period of two and half years of the Saturneffect (Shani ki Dhaiya), a planetary malfunction showed up in my son's birth chart. Along with this the conjunction of the planet Mars and the ill effect of Rahu-Ketu especially Rahu in the fourth house, doubled the trouble now. I, for instance, had become the favorite target of all malefic shootouts due to the awakening phase. And astrologically, the fourth house represents the home, stability, and family. Moon is also in the fourth house of his chart which represents our mind and also mother. So, I had to be the choicest quarry. Physical pain occurred now and then and I would find myself in bed with a bad headache or other sensitive symptoms. There never was anybody around to ask for a glass of water. My husband would be back only by late evening. As he came home tired, he hardly had the patience to notice the problem. I tried my hand at that time at various art forms that I am good at, but only to feel bored the very next day. I could concentrate on nothing and even books would not give me any interest, that I at least read. Yet, one thing that was positively growing within, was my urge to do something for myself and others who are less fortunate in this lifetime. Sometimes I would laugh at myself for such thoughts because I have always been thinking that way but ended up doing nothing so far. I had tried convincing my husband several times after marriage, to move to places where finding jobs for me would be easy. But each time he refused. Well, he had reasons that could not be overlooked too. The comfort of the job environment was his priority and so Northeast India was his preference always. Being the mandatory bread-earner he managed to get away with his decision. Self-sabotaging increased day by day and so did my frustration. The stillness all around due to the virus played a huge role in churning me from the core. I was in touch with only this one friend because he was a family to us. Although he was my friend, he was equally close to my husband and had been a teacher cum guide and mentor to my son. He kept in regular touch with us for my son's sake, so he knew my condition. He would always suggest me to get out of the house and meet people or try for a job. Being a doctor by profession he would always say that, with such emotional stress I had a risk of heart failure or would suffer from schizophrenia. He had even convinced my husband to his side. But I knew the capacity of my mind although the body is fragile. I knew if something was my strength, it was my mind and so his diagnosis sitting in a city thousands of miles away was not accountable. Yet, at times, I felt like breaking down all norms to free myself from the marooned spot. That's when one day, I had been woken up by a bird at my window. It hit the window pane so hard, that I woke up from my afternoon nap with a jerk. At first, I felt it was a sort of nuisance created by some neighbors as they tried to throw their garbage below. But in a few minutes, I felt a push from within to look outside the window. And as I did, a blackbird turned around and looked straight into my eyes as if it had to say something. I was taken aback at something so huge sitting close to me. As our eyes met, the bird flew away. But the intensity that it held in its eyes kept disturbing me for a while. At that period, social media platforms were flooded with controversial news regarding the case connected to an Actor's death in India. Everywhere, matters regarding his suicide/murder kept coming up on news channels or Twitter, also in YouTube. And due to the anguish over his death, several people expressed their opinions differently. It's this incident that introduced me all of a sudden to tarot reading. Suddenly everyone in this country became interested in knowing what the case would turn out to be and so, tarot and astrology became the most discussed topic and people followed such readers on YouTube including the ones from abroad. I came to know because, after the bird incident in my place, my social media feeds were flooded unexpectedly with such readings those days. And for the very first time, thanks to these readers, I was knowing about the Angels and became familiar with their presence even in my life. I was also interested because Kyra had mentioned the Angels. As if by magic, they were suddenly intruding on my life mystically. I started to see unusual incidents everywhere in my vicinity in so many ways. I who never noticed butterflies beyond their physical presence, started going through deeper studies on their spiritual connections and meaning. At times I would ask myself if it were only my delusional thoughts, but how could I ignore all the synchronicities in my external world and visions within my mind's eye?

In the later part of 2019, we shifted to the capital of Assam, regardless of the continuous rise of virus victims. It was near Diwali that we shifted to a rented house there. Everything was going fine until my son started expressing a strong desire to discontinue his study of medicine. To this, his father showed utter displeasure as three vital years of his life and a huge sum of money had already been invested. But my son's opinion was also not something that I could ignore. He kept saying repeatedly that he would gather no experience as a medical student and a future doctor by studying medicine online. He was to start his fourth year, out of the six, and they never had any practical classes as yet. They were taught to check BP and were learning the use of a Stethoscope, only over online classes. I too felt that this is not a sign of a bright future indeed, but could not at the same time ignore the huge monetary loss that would hit us if he decides to not pursue the course further. The communication so far was happening via me and most of the time my son would end up showing his vulnerability to me. He found it easy to express his frustration before me. My husband would not cooperate on decisions that needed to be taken. I alone could understand both their inner turmoil and conflicts and tried to build the bridge but failed. So, we could never be on the same page. Too much stress was over us because my son was still in the midst of the Virus scenario in a foreign land, far away from us. In addition to that, his sudden disliking and shocking revelation became an unpleasantry pain for us. We kept on battling over the commotion when fate played a new prank. The outbreak of war in Ukraine was in the buzz. Like the other parents, his father was also eager to wait for the crisis to settle down and then call him over. I strictly reacted this time and asked to call him back as early as possible. But things take their due time. All the airplanes to India were not open and as a result, tickets were not available. He came home just before the situation went haywire in Ukraine. A few of his batchmates got stranded there till our government took measures to bring back our citizens home, safe and sound. Yet a few lost their life. So, destiny had taken all the necessary steps to decide for us, which we simply kept lingering so far. We all should be coming to terms now, thinking that whatever needed to happen has happened. But my people were continuously brooding over the loss. There were tense situations always, within the four walls of our home, although we were trying to not communicate with each other much. The impact of the entire situation felt like stones being pelted all over me. Both were frustrated from within due to self-made issues, but hissed their anger, whenever possible, on me. Relatives were also bombarding me with all sorts of questions that were meaningless. Why was I being victimized in all this, I could not understand. Yet I took everything patiently.

I too had been struggling on my path of the spiritual bend right at this time. So, I needed my peace of mind desperately, because this is the time when one comes very close to realizing the presence of higher energies and keeps growing on the soul level. But peace for me seemed to be a 'no-no' in my reality so far. I would keep up doing the mundane works on a day-to-day basis and then would practice all that I needed to, on forwarding the spiritual journey. But it had become exhausting for me. Battling between emotional upheavals and new ventures on spiritual grounds was becoming tough to handle. My active moments in spirituality suddenly became a disgusting hindrance for everyone. Getting closer to God and His Golden Path was not taken seriously at all. Whenever I was gaining a certain knowledge regarding the upliftment of the soul process, I wanted to share my thoughts with my home mates, but very royally, I had always been either ignored or criticized. I somehow could not convince them and kept feeling low or dejected. I was continuously questioning… "why is it difficult for them to believe me?" As time passed by, and rather fast, the beautiful friendship that I so far had developed with my son, seemed to be fading away. He was suddenly growing with his own beliefs and ideologies that were different from mine. I found I could no longer communicate peacefully with anyone in my family. Not that they would misbehave, but we somehow could not come to terms with… My inner knowing, and changes in thoughts.

They almost stopped listening to me, and even if they did it was half-heartedly which led me to emotional distress and I found myself in a vulnerable condition each day. The more I started failing to share my opinion with them, the more I kept falling seriously ill. I was throwing myself into a state of believing that, being reclusive and then gradually getting bedridden, was supposed to be my said future. Meanwhile, an astrologer kept suggesting to my husband, that we follow some religious practices for my son's well-being. I was compelled to perform on his behalf as its the mother's responsibility. Practicing several rituals was not comfortable and finally, I ended up being overburdened and felt burnt out. This brought blockages on my spiritual path. A month passed and my son started looking for other streams of education now. My husband became busy with his work schedule as usual. I had been so oppressed and physically challenged, that I could not manage to walk within the four walls of my house, without support. I did not wish to talk to anyone regarding my issues at all, as my body and mind were not allowing me and as a result, I was losing good friends. Some of them tried communicating, but I would ignore them as I was too much in pain. I thought, why should I pour my negative energies on anybody and dull their life? So, I stopped taking phone calls. I avoided all social media platforms. I ended up visiting doctors frequently but nothing helped. So, one particular day, I gave up on consuming medicines which would start at the break of dawn and continued till midnight. I sat before the shrine at my home and started questioning God... "Why me? Why do I need to face the adversities all alone? Why am I the victim and how long do I need to take it?" I remember screaming at the top of my voice as I broke down emotionally. And out of anger, I started pledging that I would henceforth stop worshipping and believing in God. Having said that, I came out of the prayer room to take a rest and fell on the bed fully tired. That early afternoon, I had a lucid dream which turned my life eventually. When I hit the bed, I was so emotionally drained that I felt I would not be capable of ever walking out of the room. But here I was, wide awake and extremely happy. I shared this feeling with nobody. Since then, there was no looking back. I started practicing several rituals (not religious by nature) to what I had been intuitively guided, and I followed without fail. It was an exhausting and taxation period but I did stick to all of the events diligently without amiss. These rituals are self-acclaimed, tried, and tested, which helped me a lot.

* * * * *

THE SPRING

Although I still had been undergoing mental stress and hence felt emotionally burnt out, I realized that I was slowly entering a phase of calmness now. Earlier, I used to look out for some help, all over YouTube and even tried to follow a few motivational speakers for a week or two on various platforms. I expected to get some solace from their experience and whatever they had to share, but nothing helped. Everyone was talking about the pain and that it could be altered, but nothing much on remedy was mentioned. I was looking for… "How do we do it? How to change circumstances for good?"

Indeed, I never had the patience to read several of those religious books that are available for help or even the ones written by our famous mentors and gurus which were meant to guide us. I was not in a frame of mind to go through them at all. I needed methods that gave instant relief. So, my final resort had to be the grace of my Diksha Guru. I had been fortunate to get initiated in 2001 from RKM Order, and since then, I was only into the practice of mantra chanting. I knew nothing besides that and nor did I ever try to be more religious. I never bothered to offer any sort of puja that the priests suggest. It had been solely the mantra chanting practice so far. But now, when I could no longer bare the trauma, I had no other way but to surrender totally at the Divine feet and seek help continuously. The problem was, my Guru is no longer in his physical body. So, every single day I would almost force myself to sit for meditation after the daily ritual of puja-archana. It seemed to be the only medium that made some sense to me, that meditation would bring me answers to my situation was solace. Initially, it had been difficult. The body pain had been so unbearable that I could hardly manage to sit in crossed legged position. I would end up crying continuously, maybe for an hour sometimes. But I never gave up trying. During this period, three tarot readers out of the innumerable ones from different parts of the world helped me to maintain my sanity and I shall remain ever grateful to them. Albeit they do not know me and there is hardly a chance to ever meet them, I still express my gratification towards them and I feel strongly connected to their positive energies. Very mysteriously, when sometimes I would end up being perplexed, their general readings would pop up in my social media feeds out of nowhere, and I would get my answers through them. Sometimes some songs would just play out on YouTube, and I would be surprised because I was never surfing for them. Lo and behold, the lyrics would end up giving me some answers. This kept going on for two-three months. In the process, I got to understand that we must sit with ourselves in silence and work on our shadows. It is our inner demons that keep triggering us and making us lose our balance. I found out on my own, some sort of practices that were unusual yet conventional for me. I started helping out myself with such means and measures. I now started to understand that, the solutions for which I had been looking out and around me, were nowhere to be found externally. I had only been creating more roadblocks while trying to do so. I remember, in the days of struggle when it was becoming tough to even breathe properly, the solution is what I could not manage to find out at all by looking for it in others. I had been blaming everyone in the situation, to be responsible for putting me through such miserable conditions. Did that help? No, not till I changed my perspective. Well, considering the reality of my circumstances, many people were the supposed cause, but I gradually choose to look at things from a higher perspective. I had so far been putting my expectations on people who live with me or even afar and yet closely connected to me. I had been demanding changes and adjustments from them either silently or at times expressing myself out loud. Little did I realize then, that I was asking for some impossible tasks to work as miracles on my behalf and for my convenience. Instead, all I needed to do was work on myself and my thoughts that were in my control and in my capacity to change. It had been difficult to do so because I too had been conditioned to grow up with unnatural decisions and belief patterns that had no true meaning in life. So, I decided to take the plunge. I started questioning myself, what do I need to see beyond the clumsy and chaotic circumstances? Deep within my subconscious mind, I knew it was not my fault but blaming others was also not the solution and neither was it a sign of a mature mind. I understood that it would not help me proceed ahead peacefully by holding grudges against anyone. But the rational mind would not stop churning wrong thoughts and pushing me to wrong decisions. Thankfully, my intuition had always been very strong and I knew that Divine Blessings were to be unfolded with some tested time. So, I had to push myself further. It was going to be a tough fight for me in the reality of the matrix as well as spiritually, is what I could gather. I felt fearful about unwanted outcomes and this negative emotion knocked me out now and then, yet I kept holding firmly to my faith. My situation had become so bad by then that neither could I stay peacefully at home, nor could I be going around and out of the house all by myself because of my ailment. By the way, this horrible condition was for me alone. Nothing did change for my people despite living under the same roof. They were hardly disturbed, other than times when I disturbed them with my frequent flare-ups. Even my parental home had never been aware of any discomfort that I had been facing. To them, I am someone who could never have any issue in life that needs support and consideration. So, they never bother to ask if I am okay. I repeatedly asked God for help but could see no door opening for me. I knew it was the game of fate that simply wanted to put me through all the trials and tribulations. 'Something unusual had to be there, although unexplained at this moment...' Such thoughts would pop up in my mind randomly. I decided to face the challenges boldly. I now started asking for divine justice. I won't pretend to be all calm and composed. No, I was not peaceful as situations were not normal. I had become fearful, co-dependent, and too benevolent that it began to harm me instead. I felt helpless in every way possible and this shoved the color of despair in all aspects of my life. I realized that I was scared to such an extent, that I would not want to move out even on an auto-rickshaw, let alone use my vehicle. People whom I know and who would be traveling were not bothered about their security, but I would take the responsibility of becoming anxious for their safety. I had become so dependent, that I could never decide on food for myself at restaurants. I lost the power to even think about what I like to eat if I was ever asked. Every time I wished to buy something of my liking, I would look for a yes sign from someone in the family. I could not manage to say "no" to any demand or request that came from people, no matter who they are. I could not stop people pleasing, even when I realized that I was being used or cheated on, and taken advantage of my kindness by most of them. But trust me, even after that, I did not want to change and here I was, being pushed energetically for a massive change. The constant intuitive guidance that suggested, letting go of anything that does not work in alignment had a horrible emotional effect on me. I started asking for the situation to be positively transformed without my need to make hard decisions. But God had decided not to cooperate with me at all. So, I started taking baby steps towards the life I wanted to see for myself keeping in mind the comfort and peace for others in my surrounding. I was compelled to bring a change in my daily routine but I didn't know how to do that because a change in me means unpleasant weather in our circumstances. I knew I have to now start thinking for a future where I could stand tall in my shoes, on a much more secure ground. In the guidance that came intuitively in several forms, I was being asked to love myself. It was the only constant strong message that came along with one more and that was… "Come back to your power". I didn't get the depth of such bombarded messages initially. I couldn't decipher what I should be doing. I kept requesting clarity but in vain. So, as I sat for my daily prayers and offerings to God, I started demanding for paths to open up for me. I simply kept saying that I need help and I will not take a no for an answer. Hence, gradually I was flooded with messages which said… "Be your authentic self. Write your story, and reach out to help others. You are a Healer, a Counselor. Look at the bigger picture, see the situation from the height of an Eagle, etc."

I was devasted by all of these. Where on earth do I look for an Eagle now? And what is this about healing, I have no idea. I had been superb in counseling people always although not professionally. I did a course too but never practiced professionally. But healing? What is it and how do I go about it? don't I need a degree for that? Who on earth is going to hire me for such responsible jobs without a degree to prove my ability? I started asking out loud. I wanted to scream at whoever from the Sky was listening to me. I then somehow started to move out of the house and would walk up to a mall nearby, or some coffee houses around my vicinity and thought of writing something. I was in the worst phase of my life, almost lost in the darkness of reasoning, and here I was, planning to write. I constantly reminded myself that I was asked to be authentic and so, nothing other than what comes from a place of truth would work for me. I don't know how, but words seemed to flow out magically when I sat with the pen and paper, and within twelve days, I now had a manuscript almost complete. I had in my hand, pages on depression and how one could cope with the phenomena. It was an amazing experience indeed, though I had some upheaval moments throughout these twelve days which I spent in the public eye. I was at a total loss of control over my emotions and would end up breaking into tears for hours and didn't care that people were watching me. Anyhow, the material for my book was now ready but how do I publish it? I had been by then so helpless, that approaching anyone and asking for help with the matter, was a burden. I could not stop being influenced by something called a scarcity mindset. I was also spending the rest of the day working with my shadows which affected my emotional state of being. I knew I had to release from my inner core all the negative thoughts that I had cultivated deep within, some of which were mine and some that we carry through the bloodline by default. So, every day early in the morning and late at night it became my duty and the necessity to shed and empty myself of all that I know was not serving me. I knew within myself, that we can only let ourselves go through the process of cleansing… cleansing our mind, and hence our body and soul. The cleansing must be to tear apart my consciousness from the repels that rupture our life. We cannot try to change anyone else to experience calmness within our external reality, because universal law doesn't work that way. Meanwhile both my son and husband were adamant with their firm decision of giving me the attitude of silent treatment. They were not even aware that they were up to something which is otherwise not tolerable or acceptable and also distasteful. But they were helpless. They thought that keeping themselves tight-lipped would probably help all of us to buy time and eventually would solve my problem. But when energetic influence is what we are dealing with and when Divine intervention is at play, no human concept can be helpful. The rest of my family people also preferred ignoring it. My emotions and thinking patterns were different from the rest. I was trying my best for a year now, to be by the family's side throughout the down situations but in return, I was being treated with cold shoulders. It was a tough time to be feeling left alone in the cold but I could not pass the message to them or any other family members and close friends. I was suffering in silence because I didn't know how to bring up the matter when I also could understand that they were not directly responsible for my situation. I just could not manage to tell them- "please stop hurting me. you are only giving me emotional pain and mental distress." I understood that they were only the medium of expression through whom I am supposed to learn such lessons. The major lesson for me was to stop being the one-sided giver and I could not do it easily. I was the sole cause for becoming the victim of psychic attacks knowingly or unknowingly. It was for me to learn that I cannot allow people to be unkind towards me and that I need to voice out and say enough is enough. It was for me to learn that I have to love myself first. At times I felt like walking out of everything with self-dignity and hence adverse decisions came to my mind. But I sat with myself and kept asking repeatedly… will blaming others and lamenting over incidents that were not in any of our hands, be a real solution? Is taking the drastic step of ending one's life a solution? (As many people do when they cannot cope with the chaos), is the decision of separation or divorce the final solution? Is relocating from places that give pain, can be a solution? Each time my consciousness said… "Oh no. Not so easily. Not before knowing exactly what has to be done. Don't give up even before trying."

So, nothing in that manner was what I ever in my wildest dream, decided to do. Yes, I had felt that an end to life magically, without my trying, would be a delightful solution but

I controlled my mind from clumsy thinking. I couldn't think of ruining everything at the whim of my uncertain decisions. I have to see and go through every detail before I lose the battle of duality. I could not easily give away this one chance of rising above illusions. Not till I give it a try to see what can be changed in the situation with time. And somewhere in the corner of my heart and also in my deep knowledge, that I was now gathering spiritually, I knew this was not the only answer. With intuitive guidance, I prepared myself to do whatever had to be done. I had been slowly preparing myself to even let go of everything (including family if needed), everything that pulls me down but I have to be very sure that I am walking the right path. So, what is it that I need to do, I asked. The answer came with a blow… "walk out of situations that have run their course". Now, here came the most challenging ball in my court. Do I need to let go of everything and everyone in my life? Is this what the message means? Unable to take the pressure and stress any further, I suddenly expressed my decision of moving to Pune, to try my luck and utilize the rest of my life in doing something good. All I knew was, that there is a Healing center where I could try to enroll myself and also gather experience as a Healer. It was a shocking statement not only for my family but for myself too. I was leaping something that was out of my comfort zone. I knew nobody in Pune to decide and take such steps, yet I was determined and so within a month, I was in Pune. My son decided to join.

* * * * *

THE SUMMER

As Kyra had mentioned, Summer is supposed to be the life-changing season because the Sun is at its best self, blazing gorgeously throughout. Was it so for me? unfortunately No. Although a bit surprising, I was okay with the situation that I had come to so far because I had experienced this soul calling several times since childhood… that I need to take a step towards freedom was always there. So, I was mentally prepared.

Earlier too, I had yearned silently that my husband should take his transfer to places where I too would have the opportunity to work. But his comfort was always where he had spent his tenures and I could understand his dilemma. So, I pitched in to compromise each time. Yes, it has been a selfish move on his part but not fully intentional. All along the way, I had tried playing the role of a partner, who should be loyal and devoted to the commitment made as a wife. But then, I am also a soul on my journey and I have come to grow and ascend. So, destiny pushed me to take the leap of faith. In my mind, there were several questions. Why Pune? What am I to do now that I am here? I recalled the intuitive message of the word "Healer". I knew nothing about it, but I now forced myself to learn about it. So, the questions that arouse a tsunami within, pushed me to do something that I was least comfortable and that was asking for help. I always hesitated to ask anyone for anything since childhood. This time too it was difficult. I didn't know whom to approach. I looked online for centers but got confused and hesitant as usual. So, I started asking for help whenever I sat before the deities at home. And this was it. Within ten days, several energy healers started texting me, and some even started calling. I was amazed and at the same time nervous. What is going on and why are they trying to contact me? I interacted with two of them and it was nice to know about something so different from our usual courses. I learned about what they had to offer me, and the fees they would charge. So, one of those days when someone called me up again to join her Masterclasses, I simply declined by telling her the truth that fee structure is an issue. I cannot afford what I was asked and she politely agreed to teach me in exchange for an amount I was comfortable with and ready to pay. I shall never forget her help and the kind gesture, throughout my life. It took three months to complete the course. Well, I don't know what other healers have got to say. But this is my personal opinion that one cannot learn how to do healing until they are destined to work in such a Divine manner. No degree can testify for a healer, their ability, because it is nothing that a healer can do on their own. We can perform only when there is Higher guidance and collaboration. For me, it is a myth that healing can be learned or taught depending on the formats illustrated in the books alone. It is also very cliche to demand that healers have to prove themselves to society or the patient party, but unfortunately, Humanity still needs a piece of stamped paper to believe in the ability of the power much higher in capacity than ours. I too while holding my healing degree in hand, couldn't believe that I am now officially an energy healer. But where or on whom do I practice? My son will never cooperate. He doesn't even believe that such modalities work. I left everything for God to decide and kept thinking what else should I do? I tried approaching hospitals for work. They agreed to offer me a nine-to-five job with a salary structure that would by no means serve me with everything to maintain, from rent to social needs. My husband was bearing all expenses but I had to get out of co-dependency is all that I had in mind. I need to prove to myself that I am worth being celebrated too. At the same time, the fact that I still have to tackle each day with my son is something I couldn't overlook. The major issue between us now was not his education but my spiritual advancement. I became enmeshed in my belief in the existence of Higher mystical powers, whereas my son became a strong atheist. Three-four years into medical studies and other scientific stereotype beliefs brought that huge gap between us and a lack of understanding automatically followed. Unpleasant and uncomfortable atmosphere within the four walls raised a concern almost regularly. I thought he would gradually understand that I am only trying to help him advance in every aspect of his life. Whereas, he felt that I was neck bent on imposing spiritual principles in his life that are beyond necessity. Meanwhile, some cases of paramedical issues with clients came up for me from other cities. I started working online with a few clients as healing can be done from a distance too. I simultaneously worked with a publishing house in Delhi for that same time. Content writing as a freelancer for a short period is my first experience as a career. By now, I was getting to see some positive changes that brought confidence within me. On one occasion I did get an offer or maybe the opportunity is the right word, to work with a diagnostic center dealing with Diabetes. It is owned by a Urologist from Pune and his wife is looking into the business matter. I met her and she had been willing to help but was not ready to appoint me with a salary. She agreed to offer me a space, an OPD, and said she would try to introduce one or two patients for counseling. Her concern was, how would I manage to get clients. Yet she was open to taking me in. But then, I got cold feet because I knew no one in the city to help me bring in patients. I understood her point too. Salaried jobs were probably not available beyond certain criteria. Moreover, as she considered me to have a well-to-do background, she assumed that money is not a necessity for me and so she was not ready to offer a salary. I couldn't convince her otherwise because I couldn't be as outspoken as I was supposed to be, and failed to put forward my need to the best of my ability. I needed money for sure and that too, has to be a handsome amount because, as a spiritually advanced soul, I had a certain purpose credited to my path. I had set an intention to help my less privileged brothers and sisters who were not fortunate enough to pave for themselves a path leading them to the comfort of a shelter and good food. But I couldn't convince the same to any of my, to be benefactors. Everyone had a judgmental attitude. That I am somebody capable to carry forward my activities without demanding much for my valuable time is what they assumed.

Yet, they had expected that without fail I would dedicate my precious time to their work, which I am anyway supposed to comply with. I had two questions in my mind… "Why should I work for less pay when my time would be fully extorted? How would I manage to help the needy if I couldn't earn enough to sustain the needs?"

Even at times when I somehow convinced myself to go with it, intuitive guidance immediately followed with the bold inspiration "Do not settle for less". Since I started getting jittery, I did not accept any of the offers. Situations started to get uncomfortable in Pune now. I registered myself for a job on certain online platforms as a medical Counselor. But the calls for jobs were coming as Counselors for student admission. Well, that's not what I am meant to do. I know everyone will think why not. if I need a Job, I should be accepting anything that I can grab. Well, I need work or a job only to accomplish my soul purpose and that is, remaining authentic and helping the less privileged ones. So, I had to be cautious of what I choose to do. Why should I repeat the mistakes? Counseling a student means lying about most things that an institution would promise to offer. It means, somehow convincing a child and their parents to fall victim to the greed of huge amount settlement. No, I do not want to be a part of the night-circus. So, paying rent every month and having no income source started making me feel uncomfortable. I did start working as a healer for some clients in private but such income was not flowing in constantly. How can I keep letting my husband pay unnecessarily? It's not his spiritual calling but mine, and I have to manage on my own. So, I decided to try for Delhi and Mumbai and try harder this time. I had applied for jobs in a few companies and hospitals in these two cities before deciding to leave Pune finally. I got calls for interviews from a few of the companies and finally, a Hospital in Delhi assured me to hire, but only after fifteen-twenty days. I took everything at face value because I have never earlier had the experience of stepping into the corporate world and so, I had no idea of how it works. Happy with the thought that everything is about to change within a month, I was already in the capital city by midsummer. The idea of shifting to a new place brought renewed hope. I expected everything to go magically well. Does it seem to be so easy?

I wish it was.

But there is always the right time for everything. And I too have to wait for the right time, no matter what. So why not be more and more self-encouraging in the face of adversity? Well, that's my only, self-motivational speech that I kept repeating every day. Although the phase of my summer had not been that convincing or fruitful, the Sun seemed to be promising me the brightness I was looking for irrespective of the tremors that I knew I had to face.

I still had struggles and challenges lined up for me. By the time I reached Delhi, the Hospital that was to hire me as a counsellor, now decided to change their mind. They wanted to hire someone experienced. I was thinking, if a fresher is not given any chance, how can one ever be considered experienced? but I walked out silently. As a spiritual being experiencing human life, I look to rejections as divine protection. The house that a family friend had arranged for me, in Delhi, opened the door to surprises straight at my face. It might be a good house for most people, people who were on jobs or as students. In a place like Delhi and that too in one of the best areas, that house would have been the choice for many despite its drawbacks. But I could not consider it as a home, where I am to take all advantage of rest and rejuvenation and do healing for others through meditation. It was no less than a shabby depository, encircled by local vendors going to and from that path since early morning. Constant screaming by vendors to sell their products never made it a peaceful dwelling. Meanwhile, my son also had decided to shift with his father and this time I too appreciated the idea. I was ready for my challenges but to drag somebody into the same struggle would have been a vexation for all. By now, the tiredness that I had been intoxicated with, saw its extreme bound. After my people left for their destination, I started feeling desperate to look for a good house but felt exhausted tremendously. With no one else around to demand my attention, life suddenly turned to be too carefree. I didn't bother for food and never felt the hunger. It seemed to be a sign of despair for my friends and family, but trust me when I say that I was least bothered about my meals. I found myself sleeping till around midday and felt relaxed. This was much needed for quite a long time, is what my body understood and I felt the satiety to a soul level. I had to accept the need for the awaited rest, to function on a spontaneous spree in the journey ahead.

* * * * *

THE AUTUMN

I was mentally prepared for all the initiatives I knew I have to take ahead in life, to find my stability. With zero experience of what real struggle in a diplomatic world can be like, I had been very fanciful about the disturbing days that were to come. I thought it would be a few more days or weeks of knocking on doors here and there, and I would land somewhere befitting my ability. Well, you can't see the smile on my face at this moment, but I truly am grinning.

A series of unanticipated demur had been energetically outlined already and were waiting for me to unleash potentially. It all began with the unfolding of two paths before me. On one side, I was preparing myself to face the apprehensiveness and trepidations regarding the nature of the work I can do and how I am to achieve it. On the other hand, a new set of anarchists started infiltrating my life in various astonishing ways. Should I cry or should I laugh? had been the dilemma. Taking into consideration the very silliest matters of regular household activities, and also the very practical ones in the external field, I had to navigate my way into the calmer water of the sea with blindfolds on. So, it is clear that it had not been easy. Everyone I met at this point seemed to be prepared to teach me the callow that was wet behind my ears. Some were saying, "When in Rome, do what Romans do". They were asking me to change my personality. Some of them wanted me to even hide my identity, and become that someone whom I would fail to recognize when I look at myself in a mirror. A few were up to the pretense of befriending me. And above all, the most trustworthy friend, on whom I had been banking to receive help, who could help me to anchor my foundation on an unknown land, surprised me the most.

My goal, to me, was very clear and simple. I was determined that my purpose in life was to help humanity find its balance and ascend toward the Light-source. This is the spiritual me, very loud and awakened. So, how do I do it? was my biggest question. Sitting at home in the comfort of all the luxury is not the solution for sure. I have to plunge into the very upheaval current scenario of society, in my own way of course. I had not been trying to prove myself as a new-bee, buzzing to uphold a career or even put up a fight for one. So, there never was this smoke of competition. Yet, in my trial to express my zeal, as to what I can do to help humanity come out of anxiety and distress, I failed. Presenting my authentic self, be it during my interviews in Hospitals and Corporate sectors, or during my interactions with individuals who were in trouble, was rejected. People doubted my intentions, my capability, and to an extent my worth. They had a very unique way of saying a simple word such as, "no" in a very dramatic and twisted manner. It did smear my self-respect at times, but I vowed not to give up on my truth. People took advantage of my honesty, and my simplicity the most, when I took them at face value. I approached Doctor friends who could easily help me to reach out to the people who need emotional support and thus to my cause. They could help their patients to realize that their physical health can be safeguarded when their emotional health is taken care of. They could bridge the in-between connection and do the service of a greater cause, but they refrained. They remained silent when it came to supporting me professionally. It's not their fault. Their profession probably came on the way. They did test me by asking for healing, yet remained silent about the positive outcome because they had to satisfy their ego. They could do so, also because I had been allowing them, but not for long. At first, I got disturbed and kept thinking how could one do so? But by now, I had mastered the ability to accept harsh truths so well, that I could change my perception even faster. Well, it was not anybody's fault that I am naive. Isn't it so?... I now began to pray and ask for God's help and, Eventually, only those who were divinely guided for my help and were meant to benefit from the connection, were coming towards me.

Meanwhile, I decided to give a shape to the manuscript that I had carried with me here. Facing a lot of hindrances in this field too, I managed to get my book published and out in the public domain. My thoughts were crafted into a project of creativity when I had been in my most vulnerable and devastated state of mind and hence it is something very precious to me. This was during that painful winter period of my life when I started questioning everything and everyone, including myself and God.

I did not get the help I expected. Instead, several hurdles came by for me to stumble and fall. It was a phase of time when it seemed that everyone around me who was wearing the mask of altruism, was being exposed. I was undergoing the highs and lows that the tide of life can bring on our path. A messy situation of new people coming in, to introduce the newer game of duplicity, as well as attempts made to once again rub me in the wrong way by so-called friends from the past made me sluggish. It was only my belief in some unseen higher power of the Universe, that did come to my rescue and lifted me. Today, if I am in a position to hold myself strong both internally and externally, it is because of my faith in some supreme power that is capable to keep the entire cosmos beholding uniformly. I wonder why not a single planet or a star up there gets erratic, loses its mind, and crushes on Earth to bring disruption to our physicality. They do so, but energetically. The shift of the weather that I am using here to portray different phases of life's journey, (metaphorically of course), is for our convenience to understand that seasons do play a vital role although silently. It does teach us the patience we have lost, the kindness which we only look for in others exempting them within us, and the change we often talk about but never take the initiative to bring the same within ourselves. Today I strongly believe that my seasons of struggle were there to teach me patience.

The transition from Autumn to Winter once again, had been the most fascinating phase of experience in my life so far. I had been once again introduced to the cycle of repetitive cuts and burns of emotions related to kinship rupture. I call it fascinating because a new set of people were entering my life now yet the pattern of behavior is similar to that of old relationships. I remained that same simple soul with firm beliefs in harmonious relations and compassion. So, I trusted everyone whom I met and took them the way they showed up outwardly. I had been knowing a few people before I shifted to the capital city. I was thus confident that I am not alone in the journey. The surprise that followed in the run, shook me up totally. I had started getting the intuitive messages that tough tests are being brought in for me but I had not been aware of what is waiting to unfold. I prayed for clarity to come but this time with ease because by now I was torn apart bitterly, and was bruised all over my emotional body. How to keep dealing with mischief coming from all corners? Money had become a big issue. I was desperately wanting to earn my own and not take from my husband continuously. I had come to prove myself and do something in life. How long should I be expecting somebody else to fulfill my desires and dreams and support my purpose in life? But fate had its way. I got to work with a diagnostic center once again and had become happy, but this too closed down within three months leaving me in a back-to-pavilion state. After that frustrations went high although I knew that this would hinder my condition further. Jobs were not available for me as per my capability. My age and my inexperience in all that is needed in the sectors of the corporate world stood a barrier on my path. Each company and even Hospital needed experienced people who could motivate others to a better life. Clients were also not regular, and I already felt helpless. I asked for answers and I was intuitively told that my spiritual guides would be moving through people randomly and so I need to be aware. I didn't get at first what all that meant. Slowly, several people started to convince me that things are going to come up with time and also started to convince me to write and share needful information. Some shared quotes via WhatsApp that were surprising answers for me. All of it came randomly and I knew now what the spiritual guides had meant. These People never understood that their voices had been used to give me the answers I need. Such is the power of Supreme beings and the methods or means they use when we go through Awakening.

I had been offered jobs that were not authentic for me and I knew that these were only tests for me to see how far I had worked on myself to keep temptations at bay. My reality at present was a need for money and hence a job and so, the test was to see if I do accept jobs that had a tinge of dishonesty. Even if I would have accepted, I knew I would anyway lose the job because by now I had mastered the knowledge of the patterns of spiritual tests. To walk the spiritual path and maintain a balance in the material world is not an easy task. Only people who have walked the path and who are still walking will get what I mean to say. In such cases, Life changes drastically and so does the opinion of friends and family. It didn't take much time for people around me to change and they did, like chameleons. From the time I stepped into the city, people tried to be affable and gave a nod to our connections by giving it a name. My landlord became the honorary Father who only waited to dupe me later. A few promised to be by my side as true brothers and sisters but failed to support me when I asked for help. They chose to ignore but did not fail to say sorry though. Sorry for them is only a word of convenience, just like a false compromise used to make beneficial business deals.

On a friend's request, a known associate offered me work with her firm and promised to support me as an elder sister. So, on one such meeting, she tried to convince me to work with her but the money contrary to the workload was not appropriately offered. All through the meeting, she was only talking from a business point of view that would benefit her alone. The close friend who had accompanied us was almost forcing me to decide on her behalf. Both were doing so, to help me is what they thought. But what is my benefit? To become the victim of successful people who were trying to show their position by exercising their ego? I was in a dilemma now. I needed a job badly. The job was needed not because I had become homeless. I still belong to a well-to-do family and so, the longing for money had not been for personal or family needs. Yes, it would make me financially independent, and who doesn't desire that? But the main intention is that I have the urge to fulfill my soul-mission of serving the needy and in today's time, money is everything one needs to ask for or extend help to others. But this offer was something that was not serving my purpose. So, what should I do? They were waiting for me to say yes. I started mentally addressing my spirit guides to seek their help for the best decision. Suddenly this lady looked at the friend and said…"She will not join. She is not cut for this job. She has to be smart to instantly put a white lie on the table which she can't do. Her honesty and simplicity will come on the way". I smiled immediately because I got my answer. What no one realized was, that my guide (behind the veil) had just used her voice to put out to me the decision I needed to take. Interestingly, the lady who had promised to be by my side and keep helping me never showed up again. Friends who constantly promised to help me with job referrals, always came with proposals that were never meant for the right platforms and they knew it, yet they downplayed it. Some of them would keep saying that they will introduce people who need help in healing, but never had the time to do the needful. People who tried to become the big Daddy, got to play with emotions easily because they were trusted. My landlord who would never fail to address me as 'Beta' (my child) failed to maintain the synergy when needed. I could not live peacefully for four months at a go, despite paying huge token money to the brokers. His people chose to disturb by all means because these pranks gave them the enjoyment of seeing tenants in frustration. People who lived earlier in the same house had to suffer all such consequences each time and they left the house harassed, yet silently. The owner of the house had no code of conduct to stand tall and take appropriate actions. The Man later came up with a consoling message and expressed verbally … "Dear Daughter, I am helpless. Despite knowing that my people cheat on me often, and rob me financially, I cannot do anything to bring closure to their misdeeds. I am compelled to ignore their miscreants, as I need their assistance badly. So, I suggest as a father, that you either bare the intrusions or take a decision to shift to a better place". He was polite initially but raised commotion gradually and lost all dignity. Well, neither my rage nor my pity is what he deserves. He needs help and healing of his consciousness. I had to unwillingly leave the house but couldn't find another one at such a short duration that was within my budget. Houses that I liked and felt comfortable thinking of living there, were either too big or high on rent. Some were good and within budget but not in safe areas for me to live alone. After two months of continuous searching, I still could not manage to find a house. No matter how much I try, I will still not manage to express what difficulty and harassment I faced those days. People judged me during this phase. Family and friends who knew me for my life so far had simply decided to build an opinion that pleased them. Nobody came forward to ask me how I was doing and what made me travel away from home. They all took to see it as a reason of failed marriage and dispute. Some even went to the extent of maligning me and my intention of working for a greater cause, to be an undue advantage of freedom. They even looked at me and my connections with friends and known people at that time, with disregard. They took to consider some pristine connection to be the finagle of their obnoxious mind. I was going crazy as to what is all this happening. Why do I need to even come across people who are forcefully building up relations to only bring in their deception later? Are my past experiences not enough to prove that I have learned my lesson? lesson to never fully trust anyone from the space of the mind. A lesson to never let me put myself in a situation where I only give and not receive. I was tired and vulnerable. But slowly realized that I am only being tested, to see how I deal with the repetitions of the past activities and how skillfully I manage to sneak out of the chaos with pride and dignity. Once I got the message clear, I became now ready for every challenge I have to take but better is what I promised to make my life in the go. I started understanding that all chaotic conditions came as a hurricane only to clear my path and my mind from the confusion that disrupted my alignment with my consciousness. From this moment, my perspective changed for the better.

I don't know if anyone at all needed to hear my struggles but I know that… I am not simply writing these for entertainment. I had been urged to share my story, to help. Maybe someone out there is in need. I have so far shared only my problems but now

I want to say that these issues and several other untold barriers had come, to help me grow spiritually and be more mature. As humans, we come to this planet to enjoy life no doubt, but also to grow and evolve as a soul. Hence, although life can be wonderful and magical, it is confusing and challenging most of the time. Because this is the way the Universe tests our ability and then allows us to reach the peak of awakening and gradually the ascension follows. In a normal lifestyle too, struggles come for most people and it leaves us devastated. In very ordinary circumstances we look to put the blame on others and expect them to change. We do so because it satisfies our ego. We fail to see the issue as the "cause and effect" of repetitive actions. Even if we are not the ones responsible, our indulgence will bring certain consequences to our reality as an outcome. So, expecting others to change is foolishness. Moreover, is it possible to do so? Well, it's a big 'NO' according to me. All I understand is that we need to change ourselves to see the change in our external circumstances and for inner peace.

I too initially, in all my difficult situations, looked at everyone and considered them to be faulty. I expected them to realize their mistake and change attitudes or at least admit that they are doing wrong but to my utter dismay. I, so far, never came across someone who could understand my plight and empathize with me. No one had ever been ready to admit their fault. A few did try to help and said sorry, whereas many laughed at my condition and probably enjoyed seeing me suffer. So, can we stop them? It's pointless even to expect anything like that. The moment I realized that trying to change someone is not even universally correct, I immediately focused on changing myself. Here's what I did to work with my shadows and my agony…

Yes, we all have our inner demons and we need to banish them instead of focusing on others and what they are up to. So, the very first step I took was, to sit with myself and tried to find out all sorts of negative emotions that I have been carrying within me. I knew I would have some, so I shortlisted them. My first target was to get rid of fear. I was becoming fearful about anything and everything and as a result, I was troubling my people too. This was one of the major reasons for the indifferences with my son. Whatever I was fearful about, I had been trying to make that a reality for him. I propelled him through all of the illusions and expected him to act accordingly. This irritated him. Initially, he tried to show me the reality but with time, when he failed, he distanced himself. And I admit today, as a Healer, that he took the right decision as he needed a healthy boundary to keep his energy protected. He doesn't understand at all about energy and how it works, but his instinct has helped him to take the right decision on time. Else he would have been drained out and depleted. I took to the matter seriously now and wanted to come out of it. I questioned myself as to what is leading me to the fear. I would be scared to move out in vehicles, fearing accidents. I would be worried about earthquakes and become petrified even when everything around me is okay. I often imagined a shakeup of Mother Gaia and would be panicking. When I sat to ruminate, I found that the daily news and unnecessary content shared on social media, along with religious beliefs and the study of astronomical effects by the fanatics were one such cause. Birth charts that led to predictions of planetary ill effects and remedies by astrologers were reasons that gave unnerving attacks. So, watching unnecessary videos on YouTube, and visits to astrologers had to stop. Well, now that I understood my problem, I needed to take action on them. After a day or two, an idea came to my mind and I decided to work on it.

I am also a Healer and I know that, we as living beings, are connected with all the five elements of matter and that its complex relation holds our body together. So, my idea was to work with all the elements and five senses. I first started working on my conscious thoughts and my Chakras to heal my mind and eventually the body and other issues. I kept observing my thoughts, and whenever I found a negative pattern in what I had been thinking, I would act on the particular Chakra that seems to be associated with the negative emotion. I started healing myself and slowly my problems showed positive changes. Each Chakra, according to what we experience, shows up the result of its functionality. Is it blocked or is it balanced and energized? Everything is connected to the aftereffects of our thought patterns and when we become the slave to such thoughts that are negative in nature, our chakras get imbalanced and we manifest all blockages including a painful body. The emotional and mental bodies need guidance (not alone medicine) for sure. This side of human emotions can be helped by Counselors and mentors or Gurus and can be healed by Energy Healers and also by our efforts. It is best to take or ask for help from experienced people but be aware of fake ones. It is also possible for all to tread the path successfully with inner guidance and unshakeable belief. I strongly say so, because I am the best paradigm for my aphorism. I need to share an incident here. When my son decided to discontinue his study of medicine, I was told that he lost his mind and needed medical help. It was because he became adamant and stuck to his decision even if he lost three vital years and his father would lose a huge amount already invested. So, a friend convinced my husband to have a telephone conversation with the psychiatrist. It was during the Covid 19 period. I refused the idea bluntly and didn't sit in the two sessions where they suggested that after having a conversation with my son, they concluded that we might not get to see our child again if he is not brought back home within two days. My husband panicked at the opinion but I was too sure that he is fine. It's been three years since then and my son is still alive, still safe and healthy. So, being stressed doesn't always determine an unhealthy mind that makes one psychotic. People going through stress only needs a good listener who has patience and someone who can talk them out of a stressful situation. There are so many ways to work with our confused minds and to mention everything here, would take all my time and yours, because there are innumerable ones. But I majorly worked with the five elements and they supported me in a humongous manner. Could I free myself of my suffering?… Definitely yes. It took a few months, but I did heal my mind and then the recovery of emotions and pain-body followed eventually.

Besides Kyra, many people kept talking about the "law of manifestation", but honestly, it never worked for me in the manner that it's explained. I tried the Tesla theory and some other formulas, suggested by experienced people, but none of them worked for me. It is believed to be the best suggestion and it must have definitely worked for many, but what I understood is, if we are not at peace with our minds and emotions, then no matter how efficient the technique might be, it's not going to show result. So, the first thing one should do is come to peace with the mind and heart. We have to genuinely love ourselves for that and it is the toughest part because we look for love in everyone else but not us. We lose the power and forget to love the self because we are desperately seeking love from others. Love will come from sources one is aligned with and not from where we keep expecting. We all vibrate in energy and all we do is hold a mirror for each other. We attract connections in a manner we project us, and if we are not free of negativity, we shall project mixed emotions. Hence, love does come but with a mixture of complications and we fail to be blissful.

The youths these days are seeking soulmates and follows all sort of advice that they can gather, to find that perfect One. I want them to understand that if one is not aligned with their authentic self, one cannot become the magnet to attract true love. A soulmate is supposed to be the one who understands the partner perfectly without the other being expressive, someone who stands by through thick and thin and is perfectly suited to the other in temperament. Now if one's own energy is fragmented how can one expect to be blessed with a soulmate entry into their life? So, the first necessary step is to work on your ego and become the love in essence that you want in your life. A soulmate will enter only when you are ready. For me, the journey is different. I was not looking for anyone or anything other than desiring a peaceful life and so I took every measure possible to transform assuredly. The most difficult task is to accept our shortcomings in the situation. But the moment we do so, everything changes within us and also in our external in a positive way. Yet, I would say, it is not easy. We will be tested several times and the key is to never give up but go with the flow. People give up at the most challenging period and that's supposedly the ending phase. They give up just before winning.

In the process of shedding all negative attitudes, I learned that we also have some traumas in life that are not exactly our own. We pick them energetically from others in the family and society, from friends and the collective. Some traumas by default make an entry in our life through the bloodline. It is also a result of our belief system, and how we are conditioned to see things in certain ways because they are followed traditionally, which becomes the culprit and causes unwanted traumas. Traumas such as… inner child issues, Mother and Father wounds, Ancestral karma patterns, past life unresolved ties, bloodline issues and blockages, spells cast via dark practices, paranormal activities, etc., and these issues disturb our life tremendously. It is not the case with everyone but some people do suffer due to such baggage that might be carried from past life too or through blueprints. And these need to be released. Well, I had to deal with all these issues that seemed to be present in my reality in a tenuous way and realized that I was bestowed with the responsibility to break these negative patterns that were ruining the peace and harmony in my life. At first, I was shocked. What are all these? So, I kept asking for guidance and help, and time and again several people who know how to deal with these issues helped with the information that they gathered and whatever they had experienced. I listened to them and tried to apply them to my situation, but all I can say is, we probably do need to follow instructions but something will work positively in our situations only with mindful observation. The nature of such traumas is not similar for everyone. All of those patterns will show results for each of us differently because our issues will differ from each other. Not everyone will have a similar sort of pattern or complaint following the issues. Some of you might be interested in knowing what they are and so I will put my opinion on such issues briefly.

Trauma is a distressing experience that comes in many forms, from major life events to seemingly minor ones that create disempowering beliefs and wring up strong negative emotions. If untreated, one will carry the effects unconsciously into their physical, emotional, and energetic bodies genetically. Trauma can fragment our energy unless we release them. Once they are taken care of, we can integrate and feel whole, empowered, and free to be our best version.

Inner Child Issues: Many a time in life, we find ourselves or others have unnecessary anger issues and some even throw tantrums like a child. Many are unable to forget the past and prefer staying miserable rather than acting maturely. Some cannot let go of their past mistakes and end up remaining in constant inner conflicts that hurt them alone. They keep suffering and feeling lonely and also fear taking any sort of risk. Many again fail to see and change their habits and behavioral patterns, even though they are shown what they lack. Some do try to change but have doubts in mind and so it does not work. All of these symptoms represent the wounds that we face in childhood. These are some sort of rejection, failure, embarrassment, and guilt, that has remained unattended for a long time. This wound shows up in adulthood in various forms of low emotions and lack of self-confidence. Jealousy, anger, irritation, comparison, envy, and such type of emotions are what most people develop. The irony is that not everyone has such issues by choice. This wounded inner child issue comes from several unresolved childhood suffering of innumerable generations of ancestors and descendants. It can even become a family tradition of narcissistic behavior in one or more members detected in every generation. It is the toughest trauma that one suffers unknowingly for the whole life if not resolved. It is again the most difficult one to address and get rid of it. One gets to realize that they are troubled with such issues that are from childhood but identified only in their late adulthood. Hence to address the trauma from childhood till the present time mind frame is a heinous job when you practically will not get any help from all those who are responsible for your suffering. Because, from childhood till your adulthood, everyone responsible has outgrown that phase and forgotten their roles in shaping your psyche. But this still needs to be addressed and can be resolved with healing therapy.

A Mother wound: is a sort of trauma that is highly sensitive and not discussed much, as, it is an abuse that most women experience and struggle with in silence. This trauma, which can be a feeling of devastation, abandonment, not being loved, or unworthy of care is deeply rooted in a child's psyche. It can be so strongly rooted in wrong beliefs and confusions, that it can affect their adult relationships and mental health. It can also lead a female to have issues delivering babies. This wound can be identified with anxiety, feeling belittled, misunderstood by the mother and close family, and being pushed to a corner to an extent of incredible isolation. Self-doubt, attachment to outcomes, co-dependency, overthinking, eating disorders, and distress that lead to disorientation in regular life, compels one to call for professional support. Although not everyone suffers the same way, it can become critical and overbearing for those who felt the emotional absence of the mother from childhood. It can also be mirrored by the mother and hence the children face the same issue. It can be a projection of other female members or feminine energies (prevailing in both men and women) in the family. This can be dealt with, through a holistic approach and healing therapy. And through the process of healing, an awakening of the womb also becomes possible. One can look to the friendship of similar and like-minded women, engage in self-care practices, look for group support, and also by working towards conscious awareness.

Father Wound: is similar in nature but affects differently for men and women. As daughters, we face it in a certain way but as sons, the pattern varies. For women, the absence of a father or father figure both mentally and physically can ruin the confidence in building connections with the opposite sex. For men, growing up watching an unavailable male figure or father absenteeism whether the father is critical towards them or has abusive nature, can make them repeat the same role in the future. They can develop the emotion of rage and anger and also run away from responsibilities towards the family. One feels anxious as a child on not seeing one's father being there or giving the care that other children receive from their father or both parents. Over time, the anxiety turns into low mood and internalized anger towards the father or parents and that leads to depression for many. This results in a feeling of uncertainty and hence relationship with other men or women that they gradually keep meeting, becomes one of unreliability. They also keep attracting emotionally unavailable partners or keep giving too much into the connection that they later feel the absence of the other which leads to resentment. They either become people pleasers and hence have very loose boundaries or, they become too rigid and do not allow people to comfortably mingle around them. They often might become the victim of all sorts of abasements, or they might end up becoming control freaks. They might have a profound lack of self-acceptance and keep feeling unimportant. Many will gradually develop an unwillingness to confess the truth of their inner feelings. They will continuously feel emotionally hurt inside but will keep expressing… "I'm all right", thus leading them to mental and emotional instability, all thanks to the unavailable family. All of these are strong signs of a bloodline/generational karma pattern that needs to be broken.

There is a lot more to say on these matters and issues. Many blogs are written on these issues and many speakers are open to such topics in public forums. Addressing such issues and healing them becomes necessary. Otherwise, one can face difficulties lifelong. One might have issues with close friends, colleagues, neighbors, and mostly with partners. Most people are going through such traumas without even realizing it.

I was introduced to these traumas, that had been an onus on me, only when I entered the journey of awakening. Before this phase, everything had been fine or rather it seemed to be fine. Yes, I had always experienced the negligence and absence of my people (family in general), but I had never been bothered by the vacuum. Yet, reality can never remain untouched forever. Awakening does shake us up to an extent that it empties us of all false ego and throws reality at our faces to help us become our authentic selves. In my case, the traumas were genetic and hence a common factor in the larger family. It is a result of generational unresolved issues. For me, the overall situations and its effects were not life-threatening at all but if I have to make my own life better, I have to draw strong boundaries and break stubborn ancestral ego patterns. I also had the responsibility to break this repetitive trend of unresolved cycles. It was difficult because the old foundation that had already been comfortable for others in the family had to now be shaken up from the root to make changes. And to do so, everyone has to first understand the process, then be ready to cooperate. But my paternal family very arrogantly dismissed the whole issue. They did not even bother to get deep into the matter and simply disagreed to comply. They were meant to only help me emotionally but they denied it even before knowing what role they had to play. I had issues to deal with, that were not personal but generational stigma and it was everyone's duty to stand by me. All that a family needs to do is, support through the emotional distress that needs to be released for good. It was meant to be helpful for all but as they chose not to support me, I decided to work on my freedom alone. I cannot help others if they are reluctant because of free will. I now had to tackle the situation on a different level altogether. I decided to work on patterns that I needed to free myself from. As a result, my own family met the consequences on an extremely sharp edge. I had to distance myself totally from my kin to peacefully pull off my root from the traditional trauma bond of the family lineage. There was no choice left. I could not allow myself to keep suffering. So, to do it all by myself, the foundation within my home space shook badly. This made the situation uncomfortable for my husband and son. It was painful for them as my needs had to be prioritized instead of their ego. Yes, I had to pay heavily but for a certain period. It would not have been difficult for anyone of us, had both families been compassionate. But no one was ready to accept the reality. They could not understand that for my mental, emotional, and physical well-being, it was important for me to make necessary changes and lead a healthy life. During this period, I took a leap of faith. I went to the extent of taking the risk of even losing the family bond with my son and husband but I no longer did care. The damage done to my body was so unbearable, that I preferred to become all alone if necessary but decided not to compromise further. Ultimately, I had to take some firm steps outwardly and some measures spiritually, to bring stability into my life. We all have the right to live and that too is being equally blessed. No one person can be denied his or her birthright of a peaceful life. In my case, as I am spiritually inclined, these changes were many times intervened in a Divine way. The whole Universe had conspired to uproot the tower of a long-time establishment that was standing on a faulty foundation. The issues were not only family patterns. Some close friends and tough dealing with them were also lined up for me. To weed out the ego of false friendship and wrong attributes, was also my soul's responsibility. I seriously could take the burden no longer and surrendered asking for divine justice. And all of the actions and methods since then were divinely orchestrated. It was like participating in a marathon run to ransack my heart space. Even if it had been painful for everyone in the situation, I could not help it. People expected me to overlook matters and bring a truce to the circumstance. But what they could not understand was that it is not my doing. When spiritual activities of cleansing begin, one cannot stop or dictate the process according to comfort and choice especially when higher beings had their energy installed. As a result, those who somehow bit their lips and chose to stick by me through the storm made their voyage clear too. But those who were adamant and preferred to keep a distance lost the connective port till the next Divine Time.

Whenever a family lineage goes through difficult patterns in the family history, generation after generation, there comes a time when souls will incarnate to break this unwanted tradition and create a new cycle. A bloodline issue is not concentrated on one family alone. It includes a huge section of society because, one family that bred centuries back, has amalgamated to form one structure through innumerable branches and roots. In the family line, I am born into, similar patterns of wrongdoing that have been mentioned earlier could be seen, and I started getting intuitively that I now had to help them break the cycle. Since then, innumerable painful incidents occurred in my life and I could not manage to conduct them peacefully. Suddenly everything that the family line needs to change was shown up as a mirror to me with a similar problematic situation coming up in my life. Hence, even outsiders were projecting the typical type of relations and behavioral patterns that I could not tolerate coming from the unknown. Through dreams and intuitive messages, the ancestors were demanding freedom. But how could I help? The family line always proceeds with the male child and continues to grow in that order. And here I was dealing with family members, males of three generations who were rather trying to prove myself to be a lunatic. The Inner child issue also had been similar to many in the family but they won't even listen to what I had to say. So, all I could do was, free myself from the attacks and pain by working on some rituals that could free the ancestors to a great extent. I did a healing of my energy field and my entire body to clear all the wrong patterns that were being projected on me. It was not the ancestor's fault. They were only asking for help and when they could not get it their way, they started nudging me.

There are several methods of clearing traumas and problems in life including prevention of diseases, when we become aware of the reasons. The toughest part is identifying the patterns and issues. The ego crisis comes on the way and people defy easily. But this needs to be addressed and sorted out. I strongly recommend energy clearing that is done through holistic healing. As a Pranic healing practitioner, I can ensure successful results from this modality. There are other healing modalities too, Reiki being one, but I don't know how efficiently it works and so I cannot stand for them. As divine healing is the motive, everything should work if you believe strongly. They must be equally beneficial but one can support strongly when one has an experience. But yes, chakra healing is a necessity. One can become receptive to show sense and receive healing, even on medical grounds, only when they have a clear energy field but it has to be later maintained by vibrating on higher virtues. I personally experienced bitter times and no matter what else I did to protect my energy, nothing positive could be achieved until I started chakra cleansing. One should first find out what problem one has in life and which chakra is associated with it. One should confirm whether the chakra is blocked or overactivated and then do the healing accordingly. So, please be cautious and reach out to the right people for help. Healing cannot be done on people forcefully as the free will of the individual matters and so, energy healers are expected not to try on anybody without their permission and full concern. I did help myself and healed my problems. I am totally out of the fear and anxiety syndromes. I no longer hold grudges on anyone and nor do I suffer from resentment and anger issues now. I do not blame anyone for any sort of trouble I have to face because it's not the right way. We can never get out of a karmic loop if we hold all such lower emotions within ourselves. I choose to forgive the wrong because I don't want another lifetime of similar struggles. That does not mean that violators are free from the consequences of their actions. It's only that, I have no karmic ties with anybody to deal with lifetime after lifetime. If I do wrong then I too have to meet justice but there is a process of clearance of one's negative karma and becoming free. It is not easy though. It all depends on the realization and acceptance of the red flags.

Well, eventually I did manifest positivity, but only after a transformation of myself... my thought pattern, and my perspective. I mean total changes that are internally felt. My personality has changed to a great extent. I still am the empath and the compassionate one. This is one strong reason why I could forgive others and free myself. I still am the giver but this time onwards, it's in exchange for acceptance, respect, and acknowledgment. Those who can't respect me can stay afar. So, it has become very clear to all, that I can no longer be taken for granted. Manifestation had so forth become possible and it miraculously came into fruition even without any special technique. My strength is my faith and that increased and expanded further, making me capable to be more open to divine blessings. And just as I am writing, sitting in my room with a door and windows closed in the middle of the night, a feather out of nowhere falls on my lap. When such things happen, it's a validation for us spiritual beings, that miracles do happen when we stay close to God. My trust in divinity alone became my support system and helped me sail through, till I reached the shore.

My shadow aspects were my fear and frustration and I did overcome it. I also worked continuously to get rid of the lack mentality and win freedom over the victim mindset, and I achieved them all. I took no single medicine for the past two years. It is not because I am intolerant. I simply didn't need to so far. Also, the equation of understanding and dealings between the three of us in the family changed. Previous speculations and judgments disintegrated. Relation now is more authentic, and strong boundaries of love and respect with zero expectation and attachment are set, to protect emotional well-being. It didn't happen overnight but am fortunate that changes happened. I had to work on my shadows to change my reality. The father-son duo who had once become a major impediment on my path, is now showing positive changes. I am physically a much healthier person now. But I don't mean to say that we don't need medical help. Visiting the doctors and taking medicine on time are also equally necessary. What I am trying to convey is that medicines are supposed to aid us to recover from certain dysfunctions of the physical body but they should not become dietary essential to a healthy lifestyle. As I used several methods to mitigate wide-ranging impacts in the foreseeable and successful living organisms and wholesome lifestyles, I am sharing some of the measures taken, to bloom in adversity.

* * * * *

THE TOOLS

I did mention earlier that while working with my inner demons, I found a few mechanisms, on my own, that worked for my deliverance. So, the first thing that came to my rescue was to work with the five elements and the five senses. In the process, I started working with camphor. I would burn them up and consciously release my difficulties, one by one into that pot wherein the camphor was burning. This is an imaginary process. The aroma would spread in the room and bring calmness to my mind and body. The next thing that came in handy was the essential oils. I would use them in my bathing water mostly and would rub a few drops on my wrist, elbows, behind the earlobes, and just below the nose. They helped me soothe my nerves. JASMINE had been my favorite. Then came the potted plants. I planted a few roses and other flower plants and would spend an hour daily with them. I chose flower plants because I loved to see them grow, bear the buds and bloom someday. I would name them and engage in conversation while I watered them. They became the imaginary friends I needed desperately to share my problems. I connected emotionally to this cycle of the plants and associated them with changes that I was looking for in my life. They gave me hope each time the buds would bloom into pretty flowers. They inspired me to push myself forward on my path, with the hope that changes would someday birth a new beginning in my life. I look to my difficult period as the phase of death and transformation and a lovely way to be born again but this time into a better version of myself. This came to my help as a therapeutic tool. I would walk barefoot on the ground and feel the gentle touch of the grass. The red mud would always ease me with the cooling effect. As I did, I intended and believed that they help me release the unwanted pain that was stuck within my core. I would hug huge trees and keep breathing deep at a count of 6-3-6-3 rhythm. Six counts of inhalation, holding the breath for a count of three and releasing the breath at the count of six again. I would hold at a count of three before repeating the pattern. I did this breathing exercise thrice a day and then followed it with a few moves of the body along with some instrumental music that I enjoy. I listen a lot to drumming. The beats of the drum revived the enthusiasm within me. It brought back my strength and encouraged me to get back to the rhythm of a normal lifestyle. A few of the subliminal music helped me at times to combat the physical pain which I developed shoped due to the autoimmune disease. I honestly suggest all of these activities to my readers. Other than these, healing of the chakras and affirmations helped me the most to go through my process of dealing with the troublesome episodes.

I did practice meditation with music as a therapy. Flute and Violin are my favorites. I swayed my body in slow movements as I used touch therapy to heal the excessive pain. I kept myself busy sketching randomly. These activities calmed my mind. I know that many of you might be thinking about how all these activities can change one inwardly. I want to make it clear to my readers that, no matter how silly the methods sound they did work miraculously for me.

Being a healer myself, I did my healing and now I do help people who approach me for Counseling and Healing. Healing is a process of cleansing our energy fields which we know as AURA. It can be done distantly. A lot has been spoken about Chakras and Aura by several motivational speakers, Authors, and Tarot readers, so there is nothing much to write extra on them. Only that, I see these chakras as the gateway to healthy living. If the chakras are aligned, one can experience infinite happiness in all aspects of life, provided one maintains spiritual hygiene. Hence, for me, it is necessary to get the energy field cleansed and then maintain the purity with highly raised positive vibrations. I am a Pranic healing practitioner and if I have to mention the modality, I can say in a few lines that, it is a system of Chakra cleaning and activation of prana (life force) that helps to accelerate a human body to achieve its inborn ability to heal on its own. It helps us to live a quality life of well-being. This holistic approach is used to treat a variety of ailments, and a healer takes the help of Divine guidance and the supply of energy needed to treat the body. A healer has to invoke the Divine beings or Gods and deities, and once they come in connection with the spirit of the Divine Healing Authorities on the other side of the veil, only then can they bring the aid of healing for their patients. I see it as a sacred union and collaboration of the Divine with the patient through the healing ability of a destined healer. This is my personal opinion, and I can speak only for myself. This is a guaranteed process, for me, because I have personally healed from a pathetic condition and also helped a few others. Although they should be speaking for themselves. If one has received divine healing, then it should be acknowledged too. But yes, miracles do happen. I remember a gentleman, the father of a three-year-old child reaching out to me late one night, to seek healing for their child suffering high fever continuously for three days. At first, I took the case as a viral fever that normally lasts for three-four days. But even after healing and constant medical help when there was no sign of recovery, I became anxious. And on the fifth day during one sandhya kala muhurta, I sat to meditate on the child's healing particularly, and was given a sign of rejection. I understood it would be difficult but I needed to try once more. So, I sat for a continuous chanting of the Maha-Mrityunjay mantra through other healing processes that took me three-four hours at a stretch. Gradually in my mind's eye, I saw the child slowly recover. I did not mention anything to the family. But asked them to keep visiting the doctor and take proper medical help. I do not take the credit for any healing because I believe that, this process is showing humongous results only because the Master Healing Authorities from the Divine realm, come to perform and play a huge role in healing people. And that the ancient mantras still work magically if you believe in them strongly, was an experience of a miracle for me. Nothing would have been possible without the Divine Blessings and God's

Will. I have seen people shrug off the idea initially but come back for it, of course after thorough research. Divine Timing does matter. Everyone should do their research first because one can benefit only if they have strong faith and trust in God. Many starts judging the healer, but we are only the medium through whom Divine energy flows to reach and heal others. To believe is the right step to healing. Well, this is all I am going to point out on healing. For better understanding, you can always read about the information that is out there on several platforms.

* * * * *

AFFIRMATIONS

Besides Healing and the other means that I have mentioned earlier, I used some affirmations now and then. It did help me and this is what I would like to believe. I am very optimistic about all that I do. There are lot many videos out there on YouTube regarding affirmations. But I followed my way and affirmed my own words. It helped me. So here it goes…

First, I would pray and invoke…"Dear Divine Father-Mother God and my entire Spiritual team, my Guru, and my Ancestors of Love and Light. I call upon Your Divine presence with me and I humbly invoke You to guide and help me to receive whatever I seek for, and as I affirm, so mote it be."

1. The Divine realm supports me.
2. My Universal family loves me.
3. I have trust that all is well, and all good will be.

4. I am open to receiving help, that Universe sends my way.

5. I accept help gracefully.

6. I am enough and I love me.

7. Wisdom is innate within me.

8. I am a complete power and I embrace the magic within me.

9. I am the Light and I am Love.

10. Negativity has no other choice but to flee away from Me.

11. I am peaceful.

12. I am fearless.

13. I am joyful always within me.

14. I effortlessly manifest whatever I desire, into my reality.

15. I am limitless.

16. I follow my intuition.

17. I meditate easily.

18. I conquer challenges easily.

19. My potential to succeed is infinite.

20. I, and everyone I love and care about, are protected and safe.

I repeated (and I still do) these affirmations three times each, every single day, and always end up with a prayer of gratitude. These affirmations are auto correctors of my wrong beliefs. I now believe and find that the more I vibrate in gratification, the more I receive blessings. I always end my day with a prayer.

Prayer

Divine dear… I bow before you in full faith and convey my gratitude for showering on me your grace and blessings every single day. Without you and the divine intervention that takes place in my life whenever I need care, I would be in a devastated condition and lose my mind. It is your light that keeps me going the temple path and seeing the major clearance of toxicity that no longer serves my purpose. For this kindness and ever-loving comfort of your caressing arms, I remain an ever-grateful soul that sings divine glory. With an open mind I walk to thee and with arms open I receive your blessings wholeheartedly. I am loved and protected by your mercy. And as I will, so it be. Thank you, Dear God, thank you!

* * * *

FRUITION

All of the efforts that I had taken, did help me to change my life beautifully. Yes, it had been challenging and scary at times but I learned how to manage. When I started to deal with my fear, it took only three weeks to feel courageous and not helpless. I did overcome anger and resentment at the same time. Physical pain and discomfort took a little while but I was okay with it. You'll want to know how is it possible. Well, one has to be like a child. Children below seven years of age are not doubtful and fearful about anything because they know they will be taken care of by their parents and elders. Similarly, we have to trust in God and believe that He has our back and that we will be taken care of. The uncertainty that the changes keep bringing in is daunting, but once the outcome is there on the table, we get to realize that we were fearful unnecessarily. My journey had been tough, as there had been no one to guide me in person, and no one ready to help either. The available professional help had been beyond my capacity. I could not afford the services because I was not earning and the charges were quite high although it's legitimate considering the negativity one has to deal with through the cleansing sessions. So, I had to manage on my own. I am fortunate to have been blessed with similar abilities and so even if a bit late, I did manage to heal. It had not been just the material obstructions and physical conflicts, but also a whole lot of spiritual challenges that I had to face. Everyone, who is on a journey of ascension has to go through a tough time but the reward is extraordinary. I didn't bring up here the topics that were spiritually more challenging and advanced in nature, but the mundane ones are also not simple. They are the usual storyline that we overlook, thinking that these are silly matters. But life teaches us lessons on all simple things. We tend to make simple matters complicated. When I completed my walk through the seasons, I realized that I had been looking all along at relations and connections from a perspective that I thought to be right, when, that is not at all the reality. Rather, situations became difficult and stressful because I kept trying to hold on to several unwanted and unnecessary stories that did not serve my purpose.

I had been trying to compromise for too long with situations that demanded strong action from my side. I had been depending on my family to make a move to better the situation and help me work more comfortably on matters that needed closure. I had to accept the inner child issues that suddenly showed up. I also had to deal internally with the father-Mother wound patterns and generational trauma, all of which I had to traditionally break and complete the cycle. But due to non-cooperation I suffered some extra pain. A few of my relatives even suggested that I should visit the Psychiatrist. They focused on my demands and took them as the disorientation of my mind. Some simply took it to be my nagging attitude. So, I decided to put an end to their drama, or else, there might be a possibility that they send me to an Asylum if I push them any further. Well, it is my journey and why should the others be accommodative toward me forcefully? It is for me to have the courage to step out of my comfort zone and accomplish my purpose. They are not to be blamed because, had they known to act better, they would have agreed to sit and listen to my problem. Today when I look back, I realize that the last phase of the cycle of my four seasons ended up in a short period, although with great difficulty. Fear of the unknown took me towards a path that was full of hurdles, when, in the very first place I could have chosen a smoother path. It was only due to a matter of decision that was taken from a space of ego, that kept me stuck to several dark days. I didn't want to hurt anyone or make situations uncomfortable for the rest, but they could not collaborate. It was nobody's fault. My fear of having to leave home even if it meant for a temporary phase, became the first hurdle. It took days together to come to terms with the decision. Our Society looks upon a woman's movement and decisions on family issues, especially on marital grounds in a derogatory way. As a result, deciding to dwell in an unknown city all by myself, fear of losing money unnecessarily, the guilt of facing the unnecessary questions that came from the social hawks, etc. had torn me apart in multiple ways. I went through the death and rebirth cycle in one total year, (metaphorically I mean). But with time everything now seems easy and simple when I look back at those dark days. This happens with almost everyone who either takes the path by choice or has been chosen for it. In my opinion, if a person, place, or thing gives you pain and you want to continue with the connections, then you should give it a try. But only by working on your thought process and the way you look at the situation via a third-person perspective. Change in decision-making will become easy. Although it should be the last choice, if you want to get rid of the situation, or you are compelled to, then just distance yourself and let go in silence but with peace within and love from your heart towards yourself and others. You need to end such connections energetically with forgiveness being the prime motive. It is not a must that if you forgive someone you will have to keep them in your life without really wanting it. You forgive because you deserve a peaceful life. Forgiving others and ourselves in the situation will help us release unwanted misery and bring harmony to our life.

* * * * *

BREAKTHROUGH

At the last stage, when I was once again introduced to similar patterns that troubled my peace, I knew I had to work further with the inner self by diving deeper this time. It was once more a much detesting and terrible battle to confront and I was determined not to slip into any sort of emotional loophole. I realized that I still have some shadow sides that are buried within me. I kept holding on to these facets because I thought they were necessary to fit in, to be loved and accepted. At times when I had been attacked psychologically from all angles, I took the challenge gracefully although at certain points I broke down like a child and burst into tears publicly. People were watching me yet I couldn't help. It happened because I could not manage to handle the overflowing emotions that no longer could be stored within. There was too much pain that I needed to purge and hence I was pushed through all of the circumstances that God wanted me to walk through. I knew I was carrying the virus as a whole, I mean all the wounds that humanity gets to experience. For the common Men, it is one or two experiences for each, but here I was served the whole platter. I am one such cosmic child who had to keep following the High Orders and Guidance since childhood. All lessons that needed to be learned and carried into the DNA were properly done. But now it was the time to go through Soul-Cleansing. And it's the toughest thing to do. Why so???

Well, when all the shadows of unpleasant experiences were to be cleansed out of my system and memory, definitely without question, every individual who worked as the mirror so far had to taste the consequences along with me. It had not been a simple task. I knew what I was up to, as I was totally out of deep sleep, but for others, it was the nagging attitude of an insane me. I tried to fix the situation peacefully at first, with family, friends, and neighbors but things were going worse and bitter. So, I had to pull the final string. I started making it clear for all, that they have choices in front of them and a strong decision to take. They could choose to shed their ego, understand the truth of life beyond illusions, and change the scenario. Or, they have every right to vibrate in the false prejudices that have been conditionally bestowed upon humanity for eons. And to choose the latter, they will have to accept the ticket to a separate train that runs on a track opposite to mine. Everyone thought it to be my childish tantrum and they took it for granted that I will change within a few more months. Well, it did take a few months for me, but only to be bold and strong at decision-making. People around me remained stuck to their old selves. Hence, as they had taken their final call, my next move had to be my soul growth. I took all sorts of steps to clear the wounds of the child within me, to tear off the total skin that I need to shed. I had to release my internal pain, to heal every infectious aspect of life. In the process I lost several connections and yet I walked tall and strong toward the North-node. Those who choose to be in the mire might paint me as selfish and I gladly accept the tribute. There was no other choice for me without any support. I thought if I could stay busy with constant work, the situation would slowly become stable. But Divine Mission does not allow indecisiveness to walk hand in hand with cleansing and healing of the mind body soul. I do love my family so much, that I went the extra mile to bring a resolution but failed. I then thought that I could somehow adjust to their mindset and so I resisted for some time, the necessity to move out of the clumsy situation that had no care and affection left for me. I thought once I start earning, I would… become enough busy to be bothered with wrong attitudes. But God had other plans. And so, all ideas and hard work that I put out to make myself financially independent, went to the unseen hole. My first book, could not see the light fully. It has been appreciated but didn't reach out to the mass. A lot of painful memory is attached to the book, from its writing till its publication. People tried to deceive me in the name of help. Yet, I managed to take it to the stand. That it still didn't work, is a divine decision and I accepted it with a grain of salt. Clients who needed to heal came to me for help but at a slow pace. I felt stuck in a never moving forward situation. Nothing seemed to be working on my behalf, till I took the strong decision to let go of emotional baggage. I had to free myself from the karmic cycle that I got trapped in for quite a long time and that's what I did. With prayers intending everyone's good and with love and affection for all from an open-heart space, I released all attachments that were becoming heavy for me.

Today I feel, that had someone told me earlier that life could become easy and much merrier if we start to let go of our ego, I would have done so, ages back. Although to do that, we have to cultivate the courage that is needed and keep a check on our emotions, but then, I would have been a happier person some ten years back. It took more than a decade for me to understand the reality of life. At present, I am happy that I can look at myself, in the mirror, and proudly say that I have accomplished a part of my spiritual journey and made my soul merge with the Higher self. I am grateful for all the lessons that I have learned. And also, thanks to all who have played the role of a teacher in this complicated journey. Feelings have remained unturned considering the several wrongdoers, on the physical plane, but within myself, I have drawn a peaceful and healthy boundary with all. I am content that I could save the equation of a good relationship with the core family so far, which could otherwise have possibly gone to ruins. Although nothing is ever written on stepping stones. But I can now guarantee that if time and situations demand some adverse decision-making, I will manage to take every step willingly and in peace considering it to be "The Divine Will". And I am convinced that both the men in the situation, my son and his father, are now mentally strong and prepared to let go of the connection if needed. For they know that we will be only emotionally detached and it's fine because that's the spiritual goal. We know by now that we can be free of socially tagged relationships and yet remain soulfully connected to each other and that too with respect.

We as a collective have to realize that we need to surrender and let go of fixing situations that are impossible to manage. It is better to leave the decision in the able hands of the Almighty with full trust and faith that all will be good for everyone in the situation. It might not be exactly the way we consider as good, but it will be the best solution for each one of us. If a time comes when we have to end relationships even after hard trying, we then have to accept that these relations are not meant to walk ahead with. All that we need to do to put our effort into, is love and affection for all in whatever situation we are in. It's the essence of universal love that will put us through our hardships. I have seen two very close friends stick to their family through thick and thin. One of them had sacrificed the opportunity for better jobs to satisfy family needs. I noticed how they both stick to their principles of doing good anyway for people known or unknown, for friends and colleagues as much as they did for the family but never got the respect they deserve. But I believe that It's their kindness which shall pay off and bring them eternal peace. They have practically taught me how to love my own and others, unconditionally. Yes, Love is the key to healing and the mind is the power to wellbeing. It is that love that comes with pure intention and the mind that worries no evil.

It had been a difficult and testing time no doubt, but I managed to save myself from another phase of a karmic cycle, and at the same time I could manage to ascend as a soul in this very lifetime. I could successfully work on my shadows and manage to overcome them all. My shadows were my fear, my over-thinking pattern, my excess giving and compromising nature, and the lack of abundant mindset that I grew up with. I also had the habit of self-sabotaging and loathing. I had become codependent and accepted mentally that I could never be happy in this lifetime. For me, happiness is the inner peace that keeps my mind and body in harmony. At a certain time, I had lost my balance. But I am fortunate to be blessed and helped with all the intuitive guidance that came to me at the right time. Today I strongly believe that no one else can love me more than I shall love myself. My confidence and mental strength today do put me on a pedestal of spiritual success that I have gained. The success of bringing inner peace, the success of re-establishing a friendly and lovable connection with myself first and then with my child and family. We can now be poles apart and remain peaceful because there is mutual respect and acceptance. I can proudly admit that I am complete within me and that is all I need. I might not have achieved any materialistic success to a great extent, but then, I don't have a craving for it. I believe that as a soul, our goal should be raising our consciousness and experiencing the ecstasy of Oneness. This achievement will make progress for us and turn us to be magnets that attract material as well as spiritual success. It's the same as… buy one and get one free. I was looking forward to being financially independent so that I could help the less privileged ones. They do need our support and care. Well, although not in a huge way, I do manage to make a few of them smile time and again and that's my accomplishment.

These days most people talk about being spiritually awakened and yet get entangled and attached to the social enigma. Hence, awareness should be the first step and awakening will follow. I know someone with whom I grew up as a family. From childhood, I had this understanding that we were a close-knit family although not blood-related and so I had been addressing them accordingly. But to my utter disbelief, when I had been struggling to even breathe, this one person from the other family shattered my conditioning by saying, "Listen, you are not my sister by blood so why should I accept and support you?". It surprised me because I never approached this personality for any help at that given time. Moreover, the couple even adopted a child and this child is not their blood. I questioned myself for several days, Will they manage to do justice to their roles as parents to this child lifelong? They talk very confidently about being spiritual. Then why this feeling of indifferences? Are they even awakened to this bond between their child and them that it is not by blood? Will they still love the child unconditionally? I genuinely pray and hope so. May God bless them all. One cannot be an awakened soul if still vibrating in lower emotions. So, the death of the ego self is a necessity. Awakening brings us to the understanding and realization that everyone and everything is a part of that absolute whole and divine truth. The acceptance of totality and mere practice to remain 'one' can make someone spiritually awakened and enlightened. And to make this happen we need the mind to be a clean slate that enables us to embrace the reality of nothingness. "Please awaken to the reality of your being and the consciousness of divinity, as this is the right time for collective rising." - This is the only message I can put forth for humanity. Hope my effort to touch several souls and help each one to ascend, reaches out to the collective in divine guidance and grace.

Here on, my journey is very simple. I thrive to achieve peace and soul growth, while I work dedicatedly to be of little service to my brethren in whatever manner I shall be blessed to serve. I take no pride and no credit either, to be capable to stand by humanity. I believe I am divinely guided and hence I still can do whatever I am doing to contribute and bring happiness into each life. I only bow in gratitude, as I feel fortunate to be blessed so profoundly in this lifetime. My joy knows no bound, and I would choose to do nothing alternatively to erase the experiences that took me closer to God. I am happy that I could reach out to the 'Source of Light', and be a one with 'The One.' I am now preparing myself for the forward journey on the same spiritual mission and I am looking forward to it, with all enthusiasm. Divine Blessing keeps coming my way and that alone will allow me to accomplish my life purpose and bring the journey to fruition as a spiritual being. My gratitude for the Lord's graciousness.

I convey the message of good wishes to every other person who is walking the same path, and I pray that may you all be equally blessed. To those who are happy with the mechanical life in the material order, I hope to see you change your mind at a certain point in time, but I wish you all the very best in what you choose to be. I hope that all the means and measures provided here can help you all, to combat somewhat similar hurdles, and lead a happy and successful life. Peace be with us and blessed be the essence of humility that we hold close to our hearts.

"As I Will, So Be It, & So It Is…"

* * * * *

9 7 9 8 8 9 0 2 6 7 2 8 3